Rock
Guitar Hits

Alfred Music Publishing Co., Inc.

Los Angeles

Contributing Editor: *Andrew DuBrock*

Recordings: *Chauncey Gardiner Combo, featuring Erick Lynen on vocals (and lead guitar on "Smooth")*

Cover Photo: *50 Year Commemorative Gibson Explorer courtesy of Gibson Guitar Corp.*

Contents

Artist Index

Introduction

We all play guitar for pretty much the same reason—to play our favorite songs. It's so easy to get caught up in mastering technique, learning to read music, or understanding music theory, that we can spend hours at the instrument and still not have a good song to play. Note reading, technique, and theory are all great tools—but that's all they are. The focus of this book is to get you playing your favorite songs now! Playing your favorite songs is the single most important musical learning experience you can have. All the songs in this book use related chords, scales, techniques, and other elements, so as you learn your favorite songs, you are actually learning the skills you need to play other favorites as well.

Everything is included to help you play every song. First, there is a review of the basics, like holding the guitar and reading music and TAB. Every song is then presented with a short lesson that explores the tricks to making it easy to play. All the music is shown in standard music notation, TAB, and guitar chords so you can choose which is best for you. At the back of the book, there is a huge chord dictionary to help you play even more songs from sheet music and other books.

Most important are the recordings on the included CDs. Musicians learn by listening and imitating—the way a child learns to speak. Our included recordings allow you to learn in the most natural way possible—by listening and imitating. If you use the CDs in your CD player, you can hear sound-alike recordings of all the songs in the book. If you use the CDs in your computer and access the TNT software included on the discs, you can hear three versions of each song: a full-performance sound-alike recording, a version without vocals so you can hear the guitar parts more clearly, and a version without guitars so you can play along with the band. Listen to them often, and keep them handy as you learn each song. It's not important that you master every aspect of every song. You can focus on the parts that grab your attention the most—a lick you like, the melody, the chords, anything you *want* to play. As you gain experience, technique, and knowledge, putting the pieces together and learning the complete songs will get easier and easier. Also, the TNT software lets you loop sections for practice, slow tracks down or speed them up without changing the pitch, and even change the key. With so many tools at your disposal, you'll be able to nail any song you want in no time.

Be sure to check out the other books in this series to see if there are other favorites you'd like to learn. If you want more information on playing the guitar, reading music, or even writing your own music, there are lots of other *Complete Idiot's Guide*s to help you along.

Now tune your guitar, crank up your recordings, and dig in.

How to Use This Book

Some people approach learning an instrument by isolating all the technical skills, and, through years of study and practice, develop a command of those skills and tools. Others learn by having a friend show them a simple song, and then proceed to learn on a song-by-song basis. Some combination of the two methods is probably the best, but you should always spend a good portion of your music time learning songs that you would really love to perform for your friends and family—or for yourself.

In this book, each song is written in full music notation and TAB (tablature). Reading music is a skill acquired through diligent practice, and it has many benefits. But TAB offers a quick way of knowing what to play without having to be an accomplished music reader. We believe that providing TAB in conjunction with standard music notation is the ideal way to get you up and playing right away. Guitar chord grids indicate chord fingerings for strumming and fingerpicking accompaniment parts.

Start by picking a song you really want to play. Then listen carefully to the provided sound-alike recording (and the original version). Music is an aural art, so always have the sound of the song clearly in your head before you attempt to learn to play it on the guitar.

Read through the lesson that precedes each song and practice the music examples before attempting to play the whole song. Each lesson is broken into various sections. We've also included other info along the way to point out things that are particularly important, interesting, or helpful.

The disc and track number of the song on the included CDs. The TNT software allows access to play-along, looping, and tempo options. See the TNT instructions below.

 A brief introduction to the song.

 The main body of the lesson, with tips, pointers, excerpts, examples, and other helpful information.

GUITAR GODS

A thumbnail biography of the artist.

DEFINITION

Definitions of key terms used in the text.

TIP

Additional help, insight, and advice on topics in the lesson.

☆ **FUN FACT** ☆

Interesting trivia about the artist or the song.

If you want to know more about chords, be sure to read Appendix A. It will teach you about the different kinds of chords, how they are constructed, and what the symbols mean.

Appendix B is a diagram of the guitar fretboard, showing every note on every string up to the 12th fret.

Finally, we've provided a glossary in Appendix C that covers all the musical terms used throughout this book.

About the TNT Tone 'N' Tempo Changer Software

For complete instructions, see the *TnT ReadMe.pdf* file on your enhanced CDs.

Windows users: insert a CD into your computer, double-click on My Computer, right-click on your CD drive icon, and select Explore to locate the file.

Mac users: insert a CD into your computer and double-click on the CD icon on your desktop to locate the file.

Trademarks

Reviewing the Basics

Getting to Know Your Guitar

You may or may not be able to name all the parts of your guitar, and you may or may not need to. If you ever get into a conversation with another guitarist, however, it will probably go better if you know what is being referred to as "the nut" or "the bridge."

The Parts of the Guitar

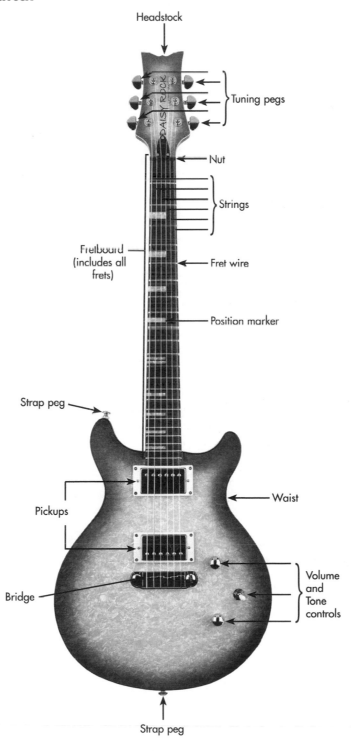

How to Hold Your Guitar

Below are two typical ways of holding your guitar. Pick the one that is most comfortable for you.

Sitting.

Standing with a strap.

Using Your Right Hand

Sometimes your right hand will play individual notes on a single string, and sometimes it will play chords using many strings. To *strum* means to play several strings by brushing quickly across them, either with a pick or with your fingers. This is the most common way of playing a chord.

Strumming with a Pick

Hold the pick between your thumb and index finger. Hold it firmly, but don't squeeze too hard.

On a *down-stroke*, strum from the lowest note of the chord to the highest note of the chord. Move mostly your wrist, not just your arm. For an *up-stroke*, strike the strings from highest to lowest.

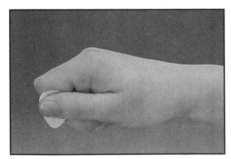

Holding the pick.

Starting near the lowest string.

Finishing near the highest string.

TIP

Strumming is done mostly from the wrist, not the arm. Use as little motion as possible. Start as close to the string as you can, and never let your hand move past the edge of the guitar.

Using Your Left Hand

Your left hand needs to be relaxed when you play. It's also important to keep your fingernails neat and trim so that your fingers will curve in just the right way, otherwise you'll hear lots of buzzing and muffling.

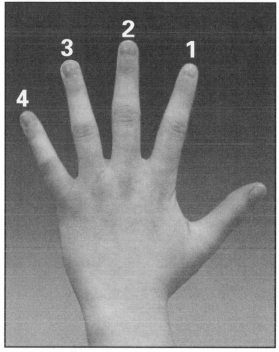

The left-hand finger numbers.

Proper Left-Hand Position

Your left-hand fingers will work best when your hand is correctly shaped and positioned. Place your hand so your thumb rests comfortably in the middle of the back of the neck and your wrist is away from the fretboard. Your fingers should be perpendicular to the fretboard.

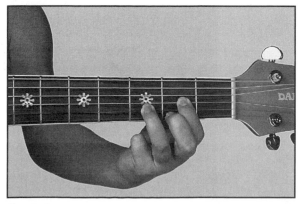

Front view.

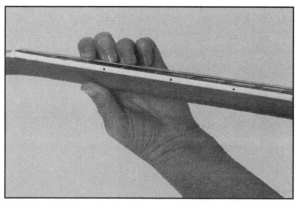

Top view.

Placing a Finger on a String

When you press a string with a left-hand finger, make sure you press firmly with the tip of your finger and as close to the fret wire as you can without actually being right on it. This will create a clean, bright tone. If your finger is too far from the fret wire, the note will buzz. If it is on top of the fret wire, you'll get a muffled, unclear sound. Also, make sure your finger stays clear of neighboring strings.

Right! The finger is close to the fret wire.

Wrong! The finger is too far from the fret wire.

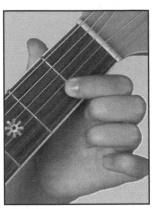

Wrong! The finger is on top of the fret wire.

Tuning Your Guitar

Every musician knows the agony of hearing an instrument that is not in tune. Always be sure to tune your guitar every time you play, and check the tuning every now and then between songs.

About the Tuning Pegs

First, make sure your strings are wound properly around the tuning pegs. They should go from the inside to the outside as shown in the illustration. Some guitars have all six tuning pegs on the same side of the headstock. If this is the case, make sure all six strings are wound the same way, from the inside out.

Turning a tuning peg clockwise makes the pitch lower. Turning a tuning peg counter-clockwise makes the pitch higher. Be sure not to tune the strings too high, or you run the risk of breaking them.

TIP

Always remember that the thinnest, highest-sounding string, the one closest to the floor, is the *1st* string. The thickest, lowest-sounding string, the one closest to the ceiling, is the *6th* string. When guitarists say "the top string," they are referring to the highest-sounding string, and "the bottom string" is the lowest-sounding string.

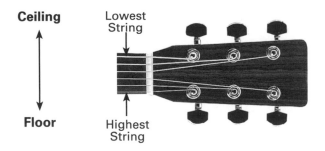

Tuning Using the Included CDs

If you pop one of the included discs into your CD player, you'll notice that the first track is a tuning track. For your convenience, both CDs have the tuning track.

The first note plucked is the 1st string, and the track continues through the 2nd, 3rd, 4th strings, and so on. So one by one, make sure the pitches of the strings on your guitar match the notes you hear on the tuning track. Just adjust your tuning pegs accordingly. It may be difficult at first, but with practice and lots of attentive listening, it'll come naturally.

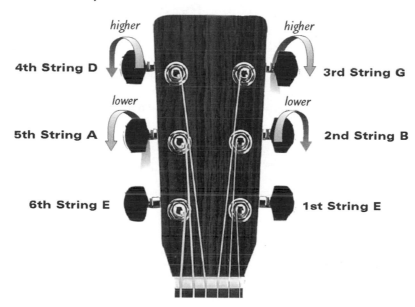

higher   *higher*

4th String D   **3rd String G**

lower   *lower*

5th String A   **2nd String B**

6th String E   **1st String E**

Tuning the Guitar to Itself

The day will surely come when your guitar is out of tune but you don't have your trusty play-along CDs with tuning tracks. If your 6th string is in tune, you can tune the rest of the strings using the guitar by itself. The easiest way to tune the 6th string is with a piano. If you don't have a piano available, consider buying an electronic tuner or pitch pipe. There are many types available, and a salesperson at your local music store can help you decide which is best for you.

If you have access to a piano, tune the 6th string to the note E below middle C.

The 6th string is tuned to E below middle C.

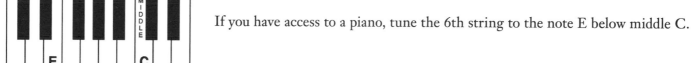

To tune the rest of the strings, follow this sequence:

- Press 5th fret of 6th string to get pitch of 5th string (A).
- Press 5th fret of 5th string to get pitch of 4th string (D).
- Press 5th fret of 4th string to get pitch of 3rd string (G).
- Press 4th fret of 3rd string to get pitch of 2nd string (B).
- Press 5th fret of 2nd string to get pitch of 1st string (E).

The Basics of Music Notation

Standard music notation contains a plethora of musical information. If you don't already read notation, you will probably benefit from studying the following fundamental concepts. Understanding even a little about reading notation can help you create a performance that is true to the original.

Notes

Notes are used to indicate musical sounds. Some notes are held long and others are short.

Note Values

whole note	o	4 beats
half note	𝅗𝅥	2 beats
quarter note	♩	1 beat
eighth note	♪	½ beat
sixteenth note	♬	¼ beat

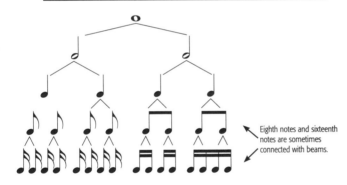

Relative note values.

When a *dot* follows a note, the length of the note is longer by one half of the note's original length.

Dotted Note Values

dotted half note	𝅗𝅥.	3 beats
dotted quarter note	♩.	1 ½ beats
dotted eighth note	♪.	¾ beat

A *triplet* is a group of three notes played in the time of two. Triplets are identified by a small numeral "3" over the note group.

Quarter-note triplet.

Rests

Rests are used to indicate musical silence.

Rest Values

whole rest	▬	4 beats
half rest	▬	2 beats
quarter rest	𝄽	1 beat
eighth rest	𝄾	½ beat
sixteenth rest	𝄿	¼ beat

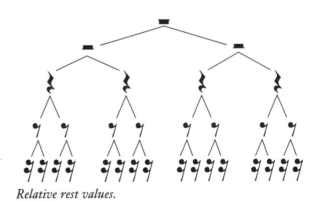

Relative rest values.

The Staff

Music is written on a *staff* made up of five lines and four spaces, numbered from the bottom up. Each line and space is designated as a different pitch.

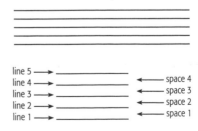

Eighth notes and sixteenth notes are sometimes connected with beams.

The staff is divided into equal units of time called *measures* or *bars*.

Measure.

A *bar line* indicates where one measure ends and another begins.

Bar line.

A *double bar line*, made of one thin line and one thick line, shows the end of a piece of music.

Double bar line.

Notes on the Staff

Notes are named using the first seven letters of the alphabet (A B C D E F G). The higher a note is on the staff, the higher its pitch.

E F G A B C D E F

The *treble clef*, also called the *G clef*, is the curly symbol you see at the beginning of each staff. The treble clef designates the second line of the staff as the note G.

G

Here are the notes on the lines of the treble staff. An easy way to remember them is with the phrase "Every Good Boy Does Fine."

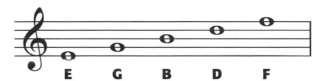

E   G   B   D   F

Notes on the lines.

Here are the notes on the spaces. They are easy to remember because they spell the word FACE.

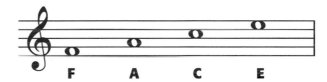

F   A   C   E

Notes on the spaces.

The staff can be extended to include even higher or lower notes by using *ledger lines*. You can think of ledger lines as small pieces of additional staff lines and spaces. The lowest note in the following figure is the open low E string of the guitar.

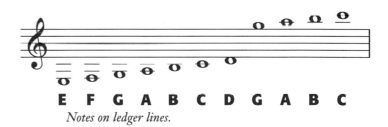

E F G A B C D G A B C
Notes on ledger lines.

Accidentals

An *accidental* raises or lowers the sound of a note. A *sharp* ♯ raises a note one *half step*, which is the distance from one fret to another. A *flat* ♭ lowers a note one half step. A *natural* ♮ cancels a sharp or a flat. An accidental remains in effect until the end of the measure, so if the same note has to be played flat or sharp again, only the first one will have the accidental. See the Guitar Fingerboard Chart on page 193 for all the flat and sharp notes on the guitar up to the 12th fret.

HALF STEPS • NO FRET BETWEEN

WHOLE STEPS • ONE FRET BETWEEN

Key Signatures

Sometimes certain notes need to be played sharp or flat throughout an entire song. In this case, it's easier to put the sharps or flats in the *key signature* instead of putting an accidental on each individual note. If you see sharps or flats at the beginning of a staff just after the treble clef, that means to play those notes sharp or flat throughout the music. The key signature can change within a song as well, so be sure to keep an eye out. Below are two examples of key signatures.

Play each F, C, and G as F♯, C♯, and G♯.

Play each B and E as B♭ and E♭.

Time Signatures

The *time signature* is a symbol resembling a fraction that appears at the beginning of the music. The top number tells you how many beats are in each measure, and the bottom number tells you what kind of note gets one beat. Most songs have the same number of beats in every measure, but the time signature can also change within a song. It's important to notice each time signature and count correctly, otherwise you could end up getting ahead in the song or falling behind.

$\frac{4}{4}$ Time

Count: 1 2 3 4   1 2 3 4   1 2 3 4

4 (top) = 4 beats to a measure
4 (bottom) = quarter note ♩ gets 1 beat

C is a time signature that means the same as $\frac{4}{4}$.

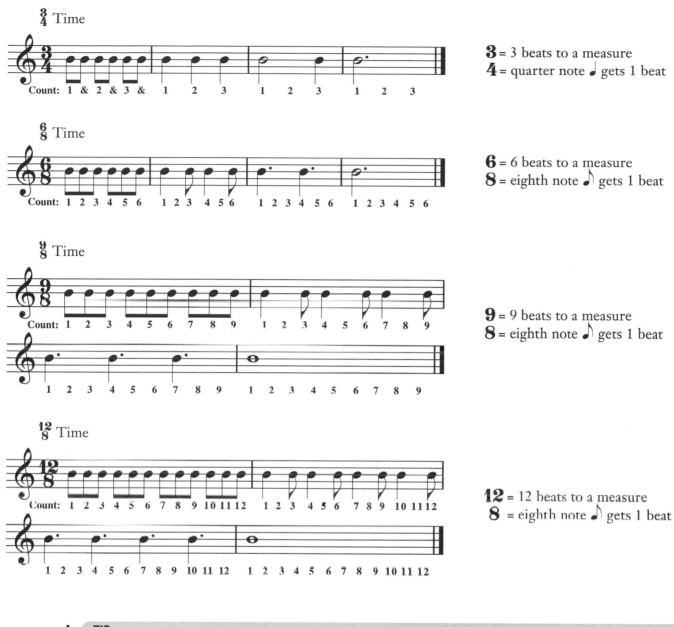

3 = 3 beats to a measure
4 = quarter note ♩ gets 1 beat

6 = 6 beats to a measure
8 = eighth note ♪ gets 1 beat

9 = 9 beats to a measure
8 = eighth note ♪ gets 1 beat

12 = 12 beats to a measure
8 = eighth note ♪ gets 1 beat

TIP

A whole rest always means rest for a whole measure. So in ¾ the rest is three beats, in 6/8 it is six beats, and so on.

Ties

A *tie* is a curved line that joins two or more notes of the same pitch, which tells you to play them as one continuous note. Instead of playing the second note, continue to hold for the combined note value. Ties make it possible to write notes that last longer than one measure, or notes with unusual values.

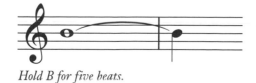

Hold B for five beats.

The Fermata

A *fermata* 𝄐 over a note means to pause, holding for about twice as long as usual.

Pause on notes with a fermata.

Repeat Signs

Most songs don't start and then ramble on in one continuous stream of thought to the end. They are constructed with sections, such as verses and choruses, that are repeated in some organized pattern. To avoid having to go through pages and pages of duplicate music, several different types of *repeat signs* are used to show what to play over again. Repeat signs act as a kind of roadmap, telling you when to go back and where to go next, navigating you through the song.

Repeat Dots

The simplest repeat sign is simply two dots on the inside of a double bar. It means to go back to the beginning and play the music over again.

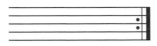

Go back and play again.

When just a section of music is to be repeated, an opposite repeat sign at the beginning of the section tells you to repeat everything in between.

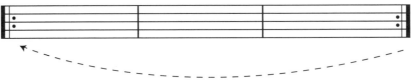

Repeat everything between facing repeat signs.

1st and 2nd Endings

When a section is repeated but the ending needs to be different, the *1st ending* shows what to play the first time, and the *2nd ending* shows what to play the second time. Play the 1st ending, repeat, then skip the 1st ending and play the 2nd ending.

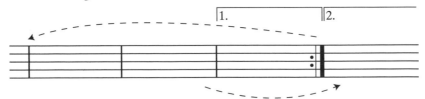

Play the 1st ending, repeat, then skip to the 2nd ending.

Other Repeat Signs

D.C. al Fine	Repeat from the beginning and end at ***Fine***.
D.C. al Coda	Repeat from the beginning and play to the coda sign ⊕, then skip to the ***Coda*** and play to the end.
D.S. al Fine	Repeat from the sign 𝄋 and end at ***Fine***.
D.S. al Coda	Repeat from the sign 𝄋 and play to the coda sign ⊕, then skip to the ***Coda*** and play to the end.

Reading Guitar Tablature (TAB)

Tablature, or *TAB* for short, is a graphic representation of the six strings of the guitar. Although standard notation tells you which notes and rhythms to play, the TAB staff tells you quickly where to finger each note on the guitar. The bottom line of the TAB staff represents the 6th string, and the top line is the 1st string. Notes and chords are indicated by the placement of fret numbers on each string.

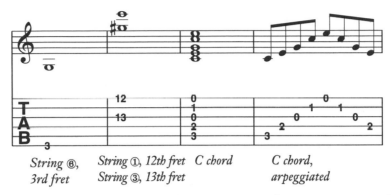

String ⑥,   *String ①, 12th fret*   *C chord*   *C chord,*
3rd fret   *String ③, 13th fret*   *arpeggiated*

The following are examples of various guitar techniques you might come across in the notation of the songs. Unless otherwise indicated, the left hand does the work for these.

Bending Notes

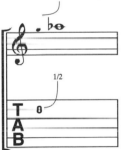

Half step: Play the note and bend the string one half step (the sound of one fret).

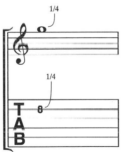

Slight bend/quarter-tone bend: Play the note and bend the string slightly sharp.

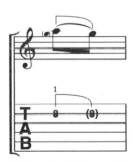

Prebend and release: Play the already-bent string, then immediately drop it down to the fretted note.

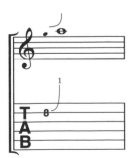

Whole step: Play the note and bend the string one whole step (the sound of two frets).

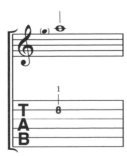

Prebend (ghost bend): Bend to the specified note before the string is plucked.

Unison bends: Play both notes and immediately bend the lower note to the same pitch as the higher note.

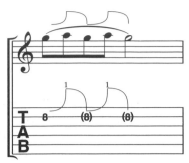

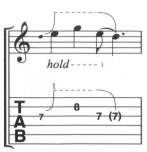

Bend and release: Play the note and bend to the next pitch, then release to the original note. Only the first note is attacked.

Bends involving more than one string: Play the note and bend the string while playing an additional note on another string. Upon release, relieve the pressure from the additional note, allowing the original note to sound alone.

Bends involving stationary notes: Play both notes and immediately bend the lower note up to pitch. Return as indicated.

Articulations

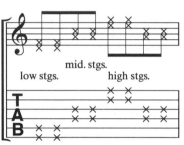

Hammer-on: Play the lower note, then "hammer" your left-hand finger onto the string to sound the higher note. Only the first note is plucked.

Muted strings: A percussive sound is produced by striking the strings with the right hand while laying the fret hand across them.

Pull-off: Play the higher note with your first finger already in position on the lower note. Pull your finger off the first note with a strong downward motion that plucks the string, sounding the lower note.

Palm mute: The notes are muted (muffled) by placing the palm of the right hand lightly on the strings, just in front of the bridge.

Legato slide: Play the first note, and with continued pressure applied to the string, slide up to the second note. The diagonal line shows that it is a slide and not a hammer-on or a pull-off.

Harmonics

Natural harmonic: Lightly touch the string with the fret hand at the note indicated in the TAB and pluck the string, producing a bell-like sound called a harmonic.

Artificial harmonic: Fret the note at the first TAB number, then use a right-hand finger to lightly touch the string at the fret indicated in parentheses (usually 12 frets higher than the fretted note), and pluck the string with an available right-hand finger or your pick.

Tremolo Bar

Specified interval: The pitch of a note or chord is lowered to the specified interval and then returned as indicated. The action of the tremolo bar is graphically represented by the peaks and valleys of the digram.

Unspecified interval: The pitch of a note or chord is lowered, usually very dramatically, until the pitch of the string becomes indeterminate.

Pick Direction

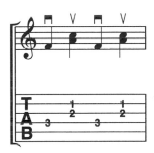

Down-strokes and up-strokes: The down-stroke is indicated with this symbol ⊓, and the up-stroke is indicated with this one ∨.

Rhythm Slashes

Strum marks with rhythm slashes: Strum with the indicated rhythm pattern. Strum marks can be located above the staff or within the staff.

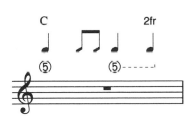

Single notes with rhythm slashes: Sometimes single notes are incorporated into a strum pattern. The note name is given, with the string number in a circle and the fret number indicated.

Songs

Another Brick in the Wall (Part II)

Key Thoughts

"Another Brick in the Wall (Part II)" is the commercial highlight of Pink Floyd's 1979 ambitious rock opera, *The Wall*. With just six lines of lyrics in the four-minute song, this minimalist Roger Waters composition is set to an insistent disco-style beat (at the request of producer Bob Ezrin) and features a trademark melodic guitar solo from David Gilmour.

Take Note

There are two guitar parts in this song. The clean electric guitar plays a repetitive rhythm during the verses, then closes the song with a terrific solo full of fluid string bends and staccato double stops. The other guitar (with distortion) closely follows the melody of the lead vocal until it opens up to whole-note power chords when the song's title is sung.

☆ FUN FACT ☆

In the mid-'60s, prior to joining Pink Floyd, David Gilmour occasionally earned extra money working as a male model. According to Gilmour, he was offered "50 quid a day to sit in a stupid motor with stupid clothes on and have your photo taken. If you could get a job like that, the equivalent of three weeks gigging, you jumped at it."

GUITAR GODS

DAVID GILMOUR is one of the few guitarists whose style is distinctive enough that you can usually identify him on a track after just a few notes. With its fluid phrasing and expressive string bends, the guitar solo on "Another Brick in the Wall (Part II)" is classic Gilmour. Though he is most often associated with a Fender Stratocaster, Gilmour employed a 1955 Gibson Les Paul Goldtop with P-90 pickups for the solo in this memorable studio recording.

Another Brick in the Wall (Part II)

Moderately ♩ = 104

Words and Music by
ROGER WATERS

*2nd time sung by children's chorus 8va.
**Tacet first two measures on repeat.

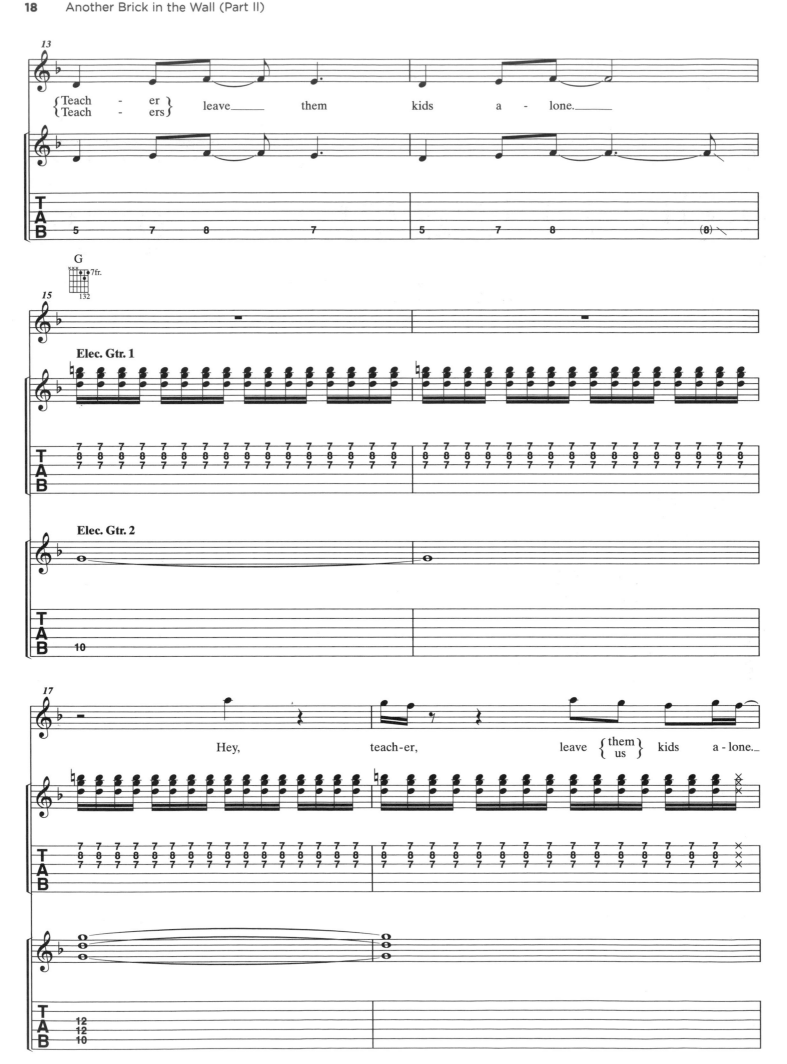

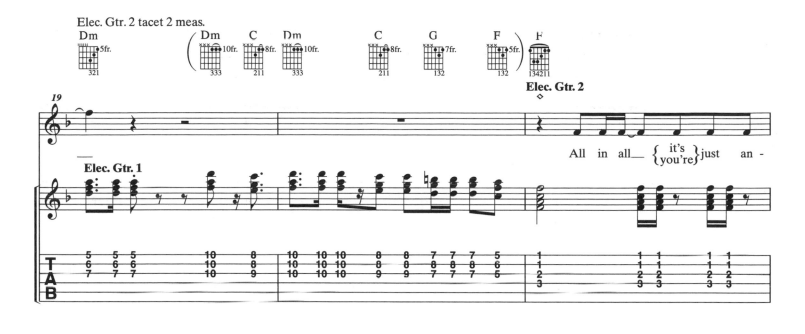

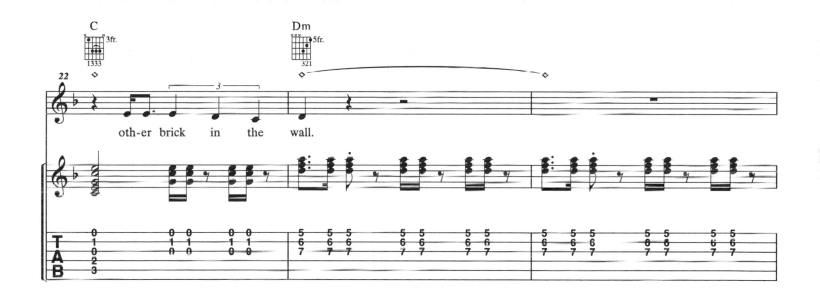

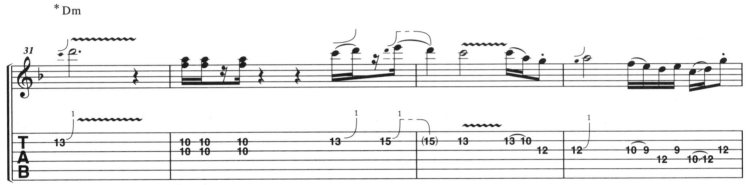

*Chords implied by keyboards.

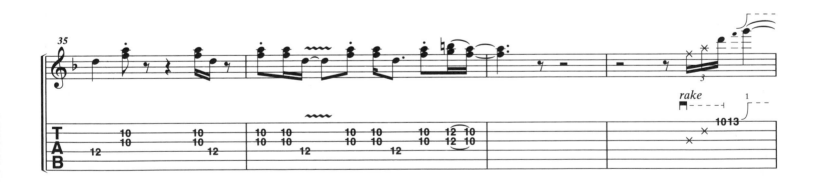

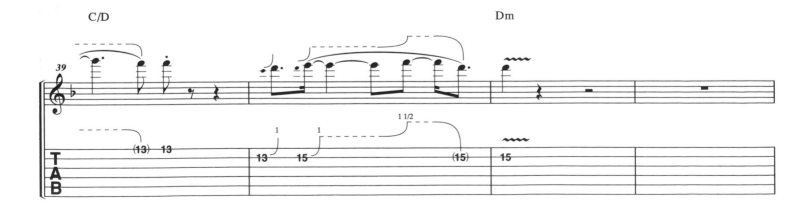

Outro: Repeat ad lib. and fade

Bad to the Bone

Key Thoughts

When George Thorogood set out to emulate the giants of blues, he set his sights particularly on the primitive blues of the "Boogie Man" John Lee Hooker. He nailed John Lee's raw, one-chord, blues-boogie sound perfectly with "Bad to the Bone."

Take Note

"Bad to the Bone" is played in *Open G tuning* with a slide bar (though you can play it without a slide). Open G is a very popular tuning that allows slide guitarists to play full chords simply by placing the slide bar across all the strings. To tune to open G, tune the 6th string down to D, an octave below the open 4th-string D. Then, tune the 5th string down to G, an octave below the open 3rd-string G. Do not change the tuning of the 4th, 3rd, and 2nd strings, but tune the 1st string down to D, an octave above the open 4th-string D.

TIP

Slides come in all shapes and sizes. The lighter your strings, the thinner and lighter your slide needs to be so that the weight of it won't press the strings down to the frets. The reverse is also true: the heavier your strings, the heavier the slide needs to be to dig tone out of the guitar. Most guitarists wear the slide on either the little finger or the ring finger.

The song is written in $\frac{12}{8}$. Technically, this means there are 12 beats per measure and an eighth note gets one beat. From a practical point of view, what you'll really feel is four strong beats per measure (where you tap your foot), with each beat subdivided into three eighth notes.

This whole song is based on a signature riff (shown below) of only three chords: G, C, and B♭. If you're using a slide, use it for the chords at the 5th and 3rd frets. To play without a slide, use a 3rd-finger barre at the 5th fret, and a 1st-finger barre at the 3rd fret. Play with an aggressive blues feel, and you've got it made.

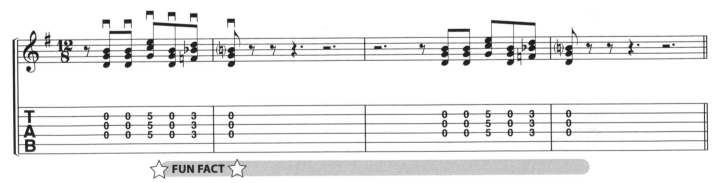

☆ FUN FACT ☆

George Thorogood was originally a minor-league baseball player, but turned his life toward music after seeing John Paul Hammond perform in 1970.

Bad to the Bone

Open G tuning:
⑥ = D ③ = G
⑤ = G ② = B
④ = D ① = D

Words and Music by
GEORGE THOROGOOD

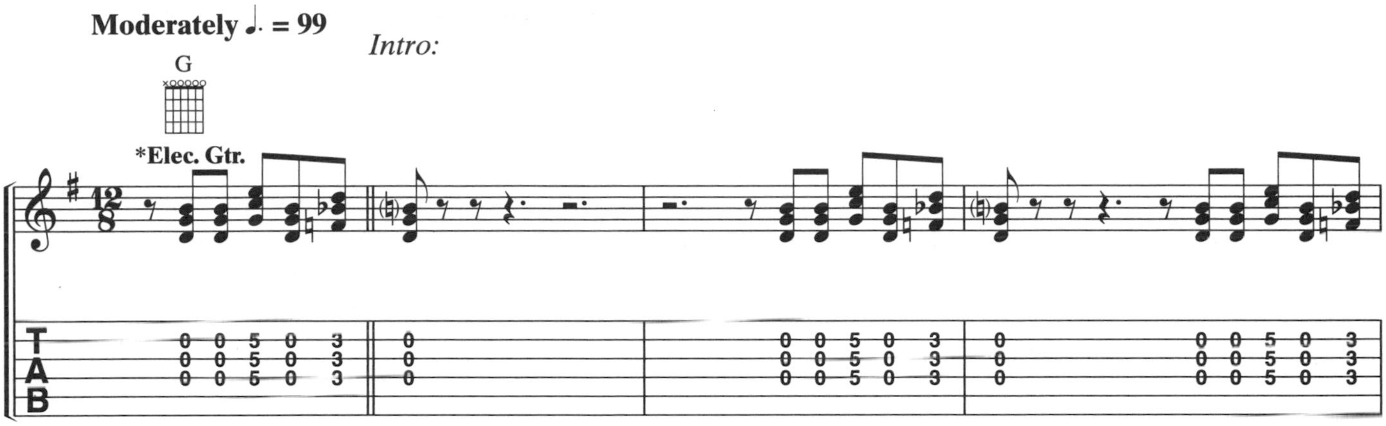
Moderately ♩. = 99
Intro:
G
*Elec. Gtr.
TAB

*Chord shapes are played with slide worn on pinky or with fingers 3 and 1.

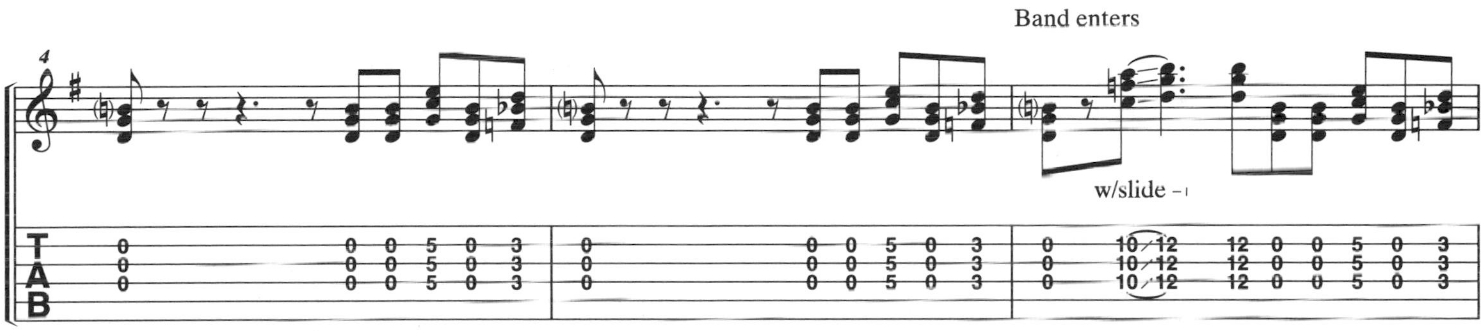
4
Band enters
w/slide
TAB

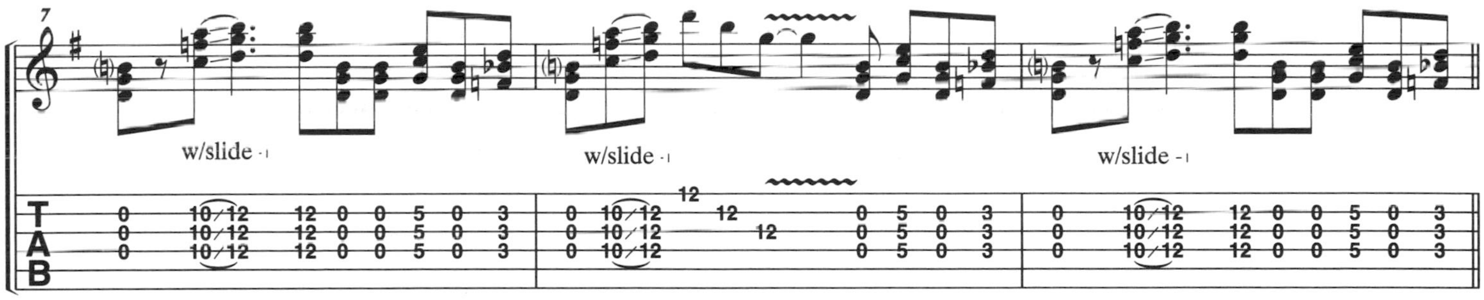
7
w/slide
w/slide
w/slide
TAB

𝄋 Verses 1, 2, & 4:

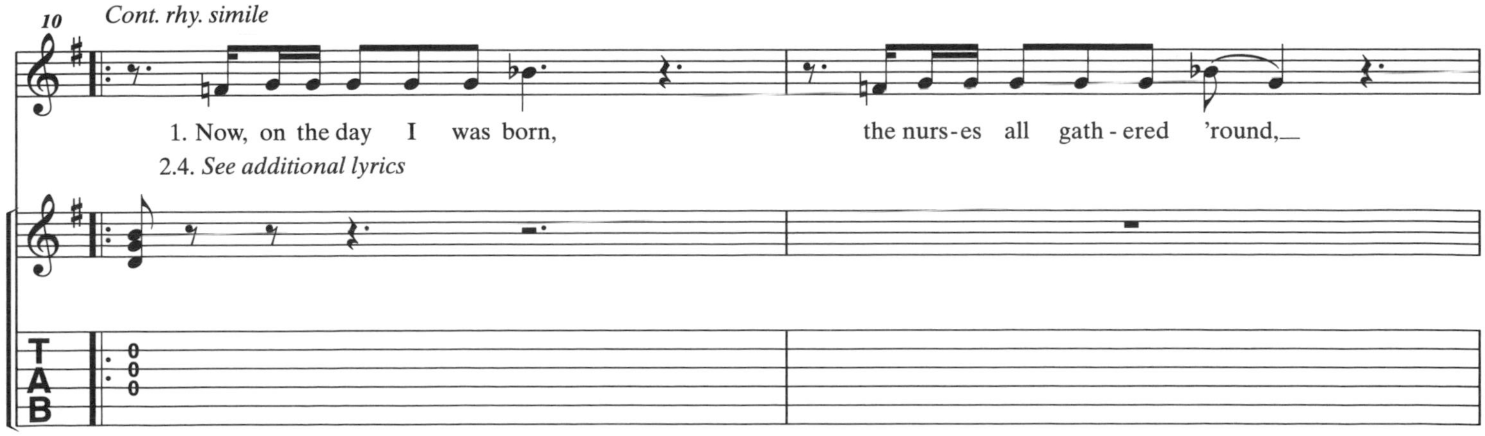
10
Cont. rhy. simile
1. Now, on the day I was born, the nurs-es all gath-ered 'round,
2.4. See additional lyrics
TAB

Verse 2:
I broke a thousand hearts
Before I met you.
I'll break a thousand more, baby,
Before I am through.
I wanna be yours, pretty baby,
Yours and yours alone.
I'm here to tell ya, honey,
That I'm bad to the bone,
Bad to the bone.
B-b-b-b-b-b-b bad,
B-b-b-b-b-b-b bad.
B b b b b-b-b bad,
Bad to the bone.
(To Guitar Solo 1:)

Verse 4:
Now, when I walk the streets,
Kings and Queens step aside.
Every woman I meet, heh, heh,
They all stay satisfied.
I wanna tell you, pretty baby,
What I see I make my own.
And I'm here to tell ya, honey,
That I'm bad to the bone,
Bad to the bone.
B-b-b-b-b-b-b bad,
B-b-b-b-b-b-b bad.
B-b-b-b-b-b-b bad,
Whoo, bad to the bone.
(To Outro:)

Can't Get Enough

Bad Company started out with a bang. Their first single, "Can't Get Enough," propelled the band's self-titled debut album all the way to the top of the charts. Penned by guitarist Mick Ralphs, "Can't Get Enough" features muscular barre chords, supercharged vocals courtesy of singer Paul Rodgers, and a memorable harmonized guitar solo.

Mick Ralphs holds down the verses with driving, rhythmic power chords. As the song progresses, pay attention to the slight embellishments he adds to his rhythm. For instance, the first measure of the chorus starts with a standard C5 power chord, but you'll need to shift your hand up two frets to grab the embellishment on beat 2 (an F triad). This is detailed in the example below. Notice the quick jump back to the standard C5 shape at the end of the measure.

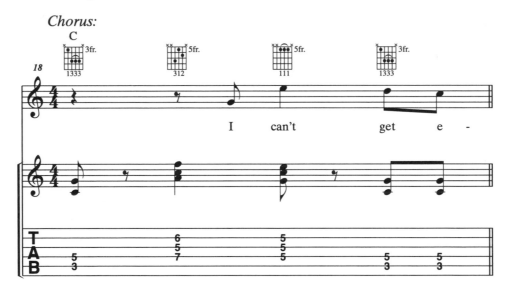

Ralphs duplicates this same move over the F5 chord in the next measure. Simply slide these chord shapes up five frets for this bar.

You'll need two lead guitarists to play the song as it was recorded. During live performances, sometimes Paul Rodgers plays one of the parts, sometimes a guest guitarist steps in (like Brian May of Queen), or sometimes Ralphs plays something completely different. On a rare occasion, Ralphs even adapts this two-guitar part for one! The simplest way to tackle the solo if you only have one guitar is to play Gtr. 3's part, which is lower than Gtr. 2, but carries more of the solo's melody.

TIP

To play the vibrato in the guitar solo (notated by a wavy line), quickly bend the string up and down repeatedly to elicit a singing tone that wavers around the note. Most rock guitarists play vibrato this way, although classical guitarists play a subtler vibrato in which the fretting finger rocks along the strings *sideways* (toward the frets).

 FUN FACT

Singer Paul Rodgers liked the 1972 Western film *Bad Company* so much that he named his band after the movie. Starring a young Jeff Bridges, *Bad Company* chronicles a group of young men who are drawn to the West as they flee the draft during the Civil War.

GUITAR GODS

BAD COMPANY was a supergroup made up entirely of members from other popular bands. Singer Paul Rodgers and drummer Simon Kirke came from Free, guitarist Mick Ralphs was a member of Mott the Hoople, and bassist Boz Burrell played in King Crimson. While their previous work helped ensure their instant success, the band went on to have a fairly extended career—especially when compared to other supergroups who only managed to release a single record before disbanding.

Can't Get Enough

Words and Music by
MICK RALPHS

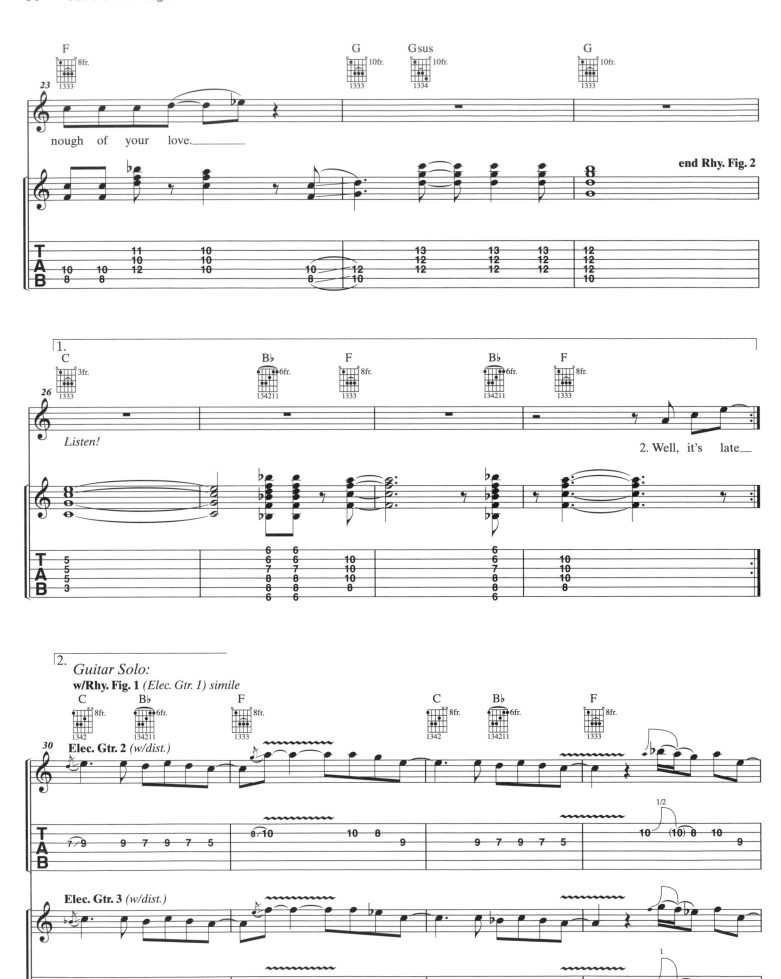

Chorus:
w/Rhy. Fig. 2 *(Elec. Gtr. 1) simile*

I can't get e - nough of your love._____ *Ow!* I can't get e -

nough of your love._____ I can't get e - nough of your love._____

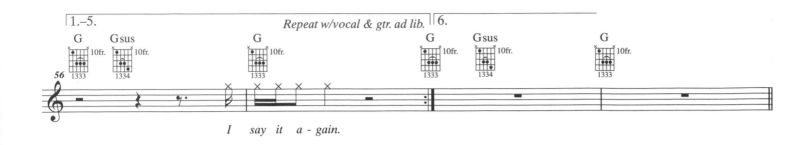

I say it a - gain.

Outro:

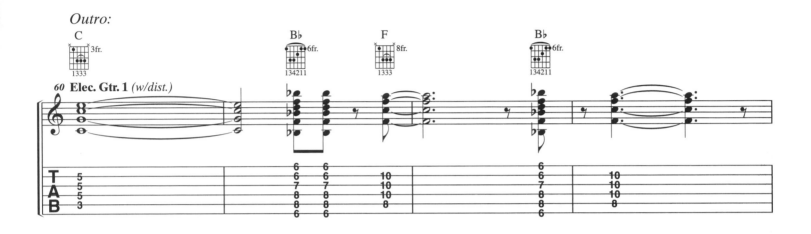

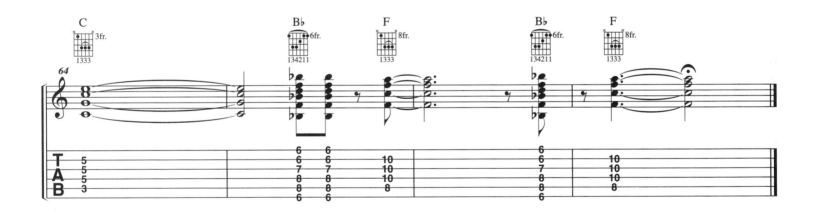

Verse 2:
Well, it's late and I want love,
Love that's gonna break me in two.
Gonna hang me up in your doorway,
Gonna hang me up like you do.
Come on, come on, come on and do it.
Come on, come on, do what you do.
Whew!
(To Chorus:)

Boulevard of Broken Dreams

Key Thoughts

No, this is not the old jazz standard from 1934. It is one of Green Day's biggest hits, though the lyrics of the two songs bear a remarkable similarity: "I walk along the street of sorrow..." (1934); "I walk a lonely road..." (2004).

Take Note

"Boulevard of Broken Dreams" was originally performed in the key of F minor, which requires the guitar player to use barre chords throughout the song. Since this might make you feel like it's the "Boulevard of Broken Hands," we've arranged it a half step lower, in the key of E minor. If you want to play along with the recording, just put a capo at the 1st fret and play the song as shown here.

The rhythm pattern for the verse is transcribed below. Follow the strumming directions, and notice there is a muted stroke (indicated by an "x" notehead) just before each chord transition. This muted stroke gives your hand a moment to change position.

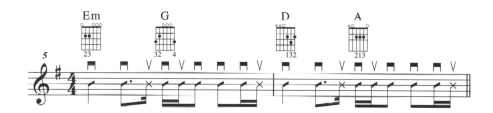

For the chorus, the rhythm changes to straight eighth notes. Use all down-strokes in this section.

The outro figure at bar 52 takes an unexpected turn in the form of the D♯5 chord, which acts as a leading tone back to the Em chord. The song's abrupt ending on the D♯5 is jarring and leaves the listener waiting for a resolution that never comes.

GUITAR GODS

GREEN DAY's *American Idiot* earned great critical acclaim. The album touched on timely issues of the day and featured singles like "American Idiot," "Boulevard of Broken Dreams," "Holiday," and "Wake Me Up When September Ends." *American Idiot* received seven Grammy nominations, eventually winning the Best Rock Album award.

Boulevard of Broken Dreams

To match record key, Capo I

Words by BILLIE JOE
Music by GREEN DAY

Guitar Solo:

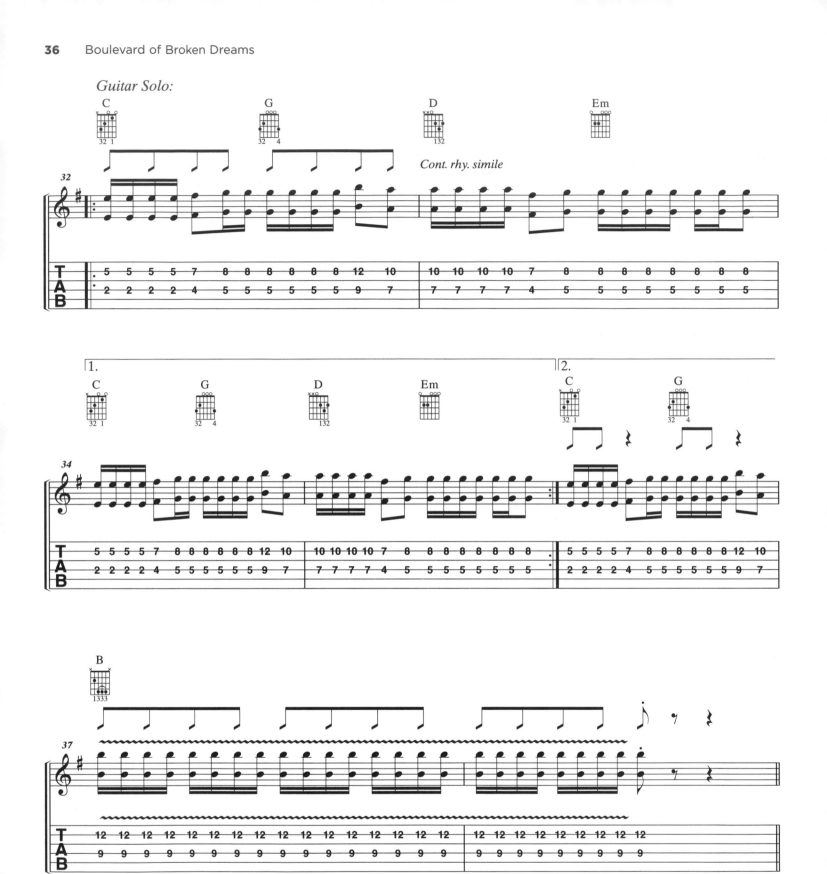

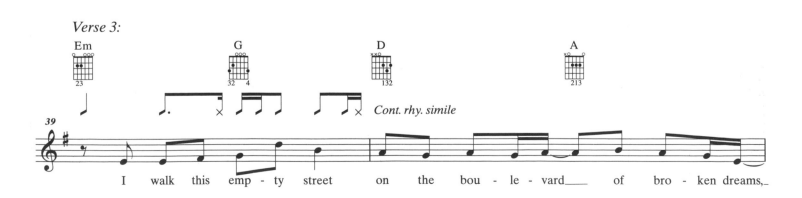

I walk this emp-ty street on the bou-le-vard___ of bro-ken dreams,___

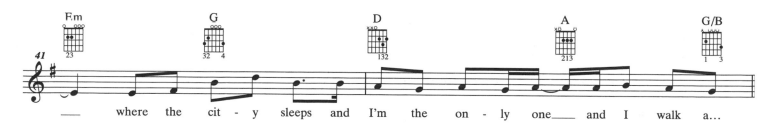

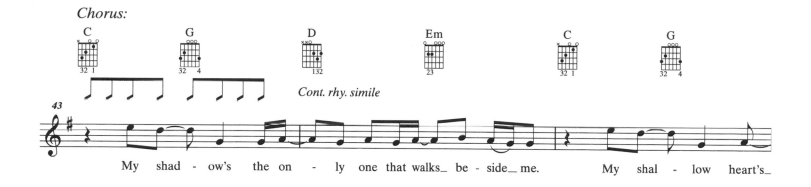

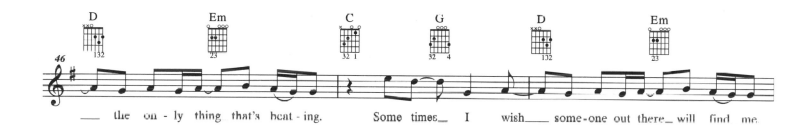

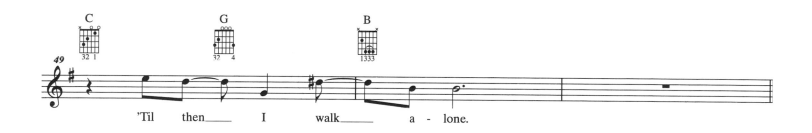

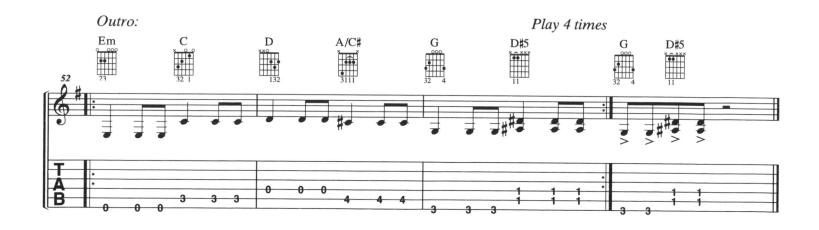

China Grove

A top-20 hit from The Doobie Brothers' third album, "China Grove" has been a staple on classic rock radio since its release in 1973.

The basic riff, Rhy. Fig. 1, requires some deft string muting between accented chords. Mutes are indicated with "x" noteheads in the transcription. Play the two E chords at the 7th fret with down-strokes. Now, after a quick downward slide, return your hand to the 7th-fret position, and slightly lift your fingers from the fretboard while continuing to make contact with the strings. This will muffle the strings to produce a dull, percussive sound without a distinct pitch when you strum. You'll need to raise your index finger up a little from the E chord to mute the 6th string as well.

In measure 3, move your left hand down to the D5 chord at the 5th fret. Keep your pick hand moving down and up in a constant eighth-note motion for this measure. Strike D5 on beat 1, play muted strokes on the "&" of 1 and the downbeat of 2, then catch the A/C♯ chord with the up-stroke on the "&" of 2. Play muted strokes on 3 and "&," move to the open-position A5 chord to play a down-stroke on beat 4 and a muted up-stroke on the "&," then quickly move back to the 7th fret for a return to the E chord. This rhythmic motif carries through both the verse and chorus.

TIP

The "&" of a beat is the second half of the beat, as when counting eighth notes:
1 & 2 & 3 & 4 & . . .

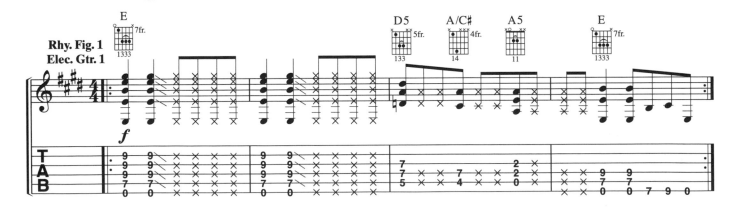

The next example shows the rhythm from the two-beat pickup into the bridge.

Continue this basic rhythm strum pattern until the C–D–E progression, which leads back to the verse pattern. We've thrown in an optional lead guitar fill after the first E chord, but if you prefer, you can let the E chord sustain across the measure instead.

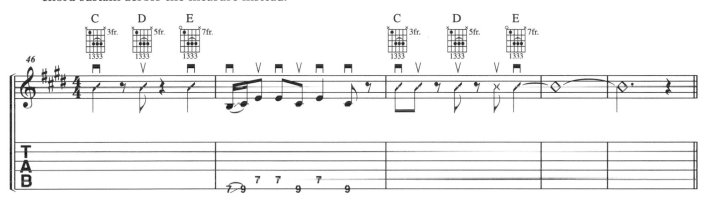

The solo (beginning in measure 54) tastefully blends both the major pentatonic (E–F#–G#–B–C#) and minor pentatonic (E–G–A–B–D) scales.

☆ **FUN FACT** ☆

Tom Johnston's lyrics contain an ill-informed reference to samurai swords, which are actually Japanese, not Chinese, and would not likely be found in "China" Grove.

GUITAR GODS

THE DOOBIE BROTHERS recorded some of the biggest hits of the 1970s, giving us classic rock staples like "Black Water," "Long Train Runnin'," and "What a Fool Believes." Starting out as a Northern California country-boogie band, they were constantly evolving and covered lots of musical ground in their career, crafting songs that melded rock, country, boogie, R&B, light funk, pop, and jazz. Interestingly, among their staunchest supporters in the early days was outlaw biker gang the Hell's Angels. But as the band's sound evolved, so did its fan base. The Doobie Brothers' breakthrough album was *Toulouse Street,* released in 1972, which includes the classics "Rockin' Down the Highway," "Jesus Is Just Alright," and "Listen to the Music." Their 1973 follow-up, *The Captain and Me,* was an even bigger success and features the hit "China Grove." Over their 40-year career, The Doobie Brothers have had many band members, but Patrick Simmons and Tom Johnston continue to carry the flame that keeps the Doobies burnin' and rockin' down the highway.

China Grove

Words and Music by
TOM JOHNSTON

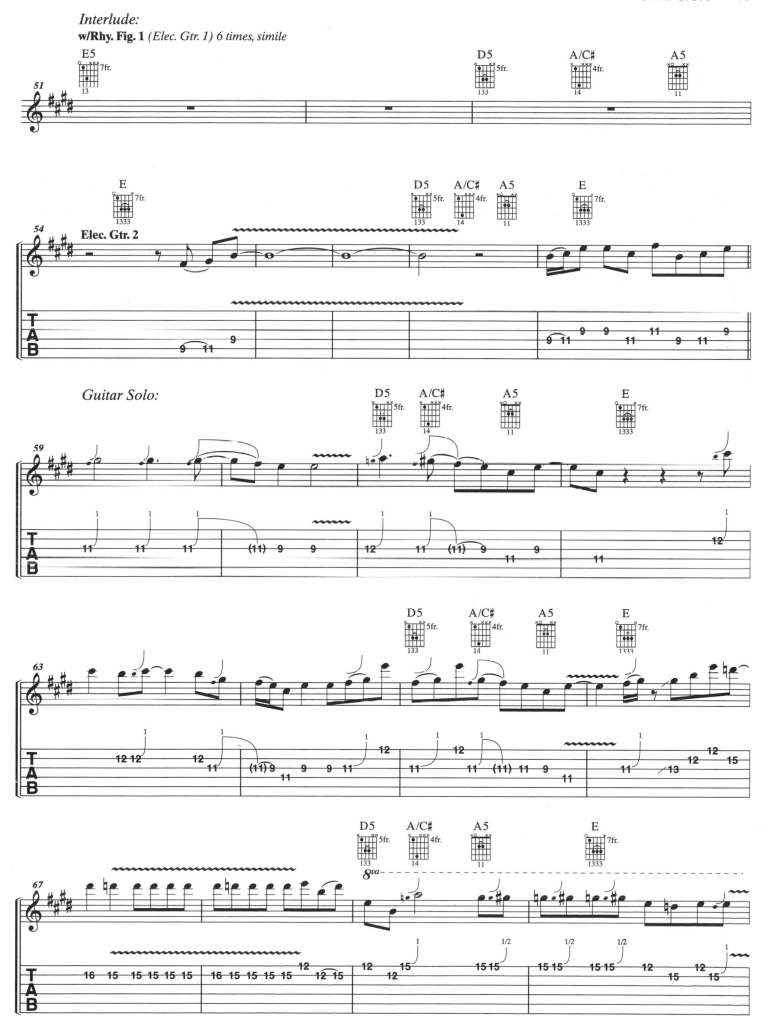

Cocaine

Key Thoughts

Eric Clapton was already a guitar hero by the time he went solo in 1970 and released his self-titled debut album. But it wasn't until he released *Slowhand* in 1977 that he hit his stride as a solo artist. Behind the strength of three huge songs—"Lay Down Sally," "Wonderful Tonight," and "Cocaine"—*Slowhand* climbed all the way to No. 2 on *Billboard*'s Top 200 album chart. "Cocaine," the leadoff track, is a cover of a J. J. Cale song. Clapton's take on the tune is similar to Cale's, except that Clapton moved the song up from the key of D♭ to the key of E.

Take Note

Clapton builds most of the rhythm guitar part by sliding a single barre chord shape up and down the neck. He spices this up with a second guitar part (shown in notation and TAB) to add fills between these chord shapes. Pay attention to the *syncopated* chords in measures 26–27.

DEFINITION

Syncopation occurs when weak beats are accented in a rhythm. The chords at the end of the verse in "Cocaine" are a great example of syncopation.

Clapton creates a memorable guitar solo by navigating through just one position of the E minor pentatonic scale.

E Minor Pentatonic Scale

Of course, simply running up and down this scale won't create a great solo. Listen closely to the original recording or the provided sound-alike version; what makes Clapton's lines memorable is his mastery of the nuances—bends, vibrato, double stops, and hammer-ons and pull-offs.

For the unison bends in measures 27–28, fret the 12th fret of the 2nd string with your index finger, and bend the note at the 14th fret of the 3rd string up with your ring finger—backing that up with your middle finger. The word "unison" refers to the fact that more than one note is the same pitch; in unison bends, a bent note doubles another played note.

 FUN FACT

"Cocaine" appears on *Slowhand*, an album titled after the nickname Yardbirds manager Giorgio Gomelsky gave to Eric Clapton. During his Yardbird days, if Clapton broke a string onstage, he'd take a long time to re-string his guitar—while the audience patiently waited, clapping slowly. Gomelsky turned this image into Clapton's nickname: Slowhand.

 **GUITAR GODS**

ERIC CLAPTON sits at the apex of all guitar gods. Starting his career as a member of the Yardbirds, he later worked with the Bluesbreakers, then saw huge success as a member of Cream. After a quick stint with another supergroup—Blind Faith—Clapton emerged as a solo artist. Right around this time, Clapton also launched Derek & the Dominos, a group that featured some of his best work ("Layla") alongside another legendary guitarist—Duane Allman. As Clapton became more comfortable in his solo role through records like *Slowhand* and *Backless*, his breadth of work expanded, and he released the hugely successful *Unplugged* in the '90s as well as the tribute records to his blues heroes *From the Cradle* and *Me and Mr. Johnson*. From early in his career, Clapton has been one of the largest icons in rock music. He was still a fairly young guitarist with the Bluesbreakers when an admirer spray-painted the legendary slogan "Clapton is God" on a wall in the London Underground.

Cocaine

Moderate rock ♩ = 106

Words and Music by
J.J. CALE

Intro:

Creep

"Creep" put Radiohead on the international map, but it wasn't an overnight success. Included on the band's 1993 debut record *Pablo Honey*, "Creep" was released as a single the year before, but the song didn't start climbing the charts until several months after the album hit the shelves. The success of the song pushed *Pablo Honey* to No. 32 on *Billboard*'s Top 200 album chart.

Take Note

Throughout the intro and verses, guitarist Ed O'Brien helps create a psychedelic backdrop by *arpeggiating* chord shapes. (If you're unfamiliar with arpeggios, see the definition in the lesson for "Hotel California.") You can pick these notes a variety of ways. One way is by using alternate picking, which alternates between down-strokes and up-strokes for each consecutive eighth note. You could also try economy picking, which aims for an economy of motion in every stroke—a technique that creates more fluid motion, but less consistent picking patterns. Try both techniques in the example below. In this passage, the majority of guitarists would probably use economy picking, but you should use the technique that feels most comfortable.

TIP

Any time you play the notes of a chord individually, you're playing an arpeggio. To arpeggiate a chord, just play the individual notes in any order. All arpeggios are built from single notes; once you play two or more notes at the same time, you're no longer playing an arpeggio.

Intro:

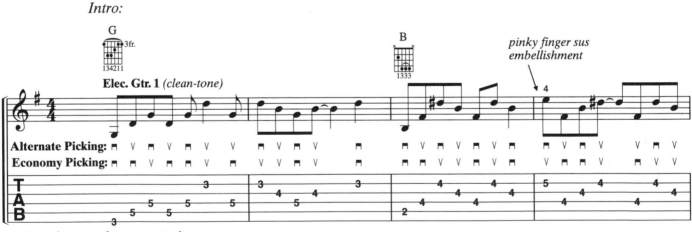

* ⊓ = down-stroke; ∨ = up-stroke

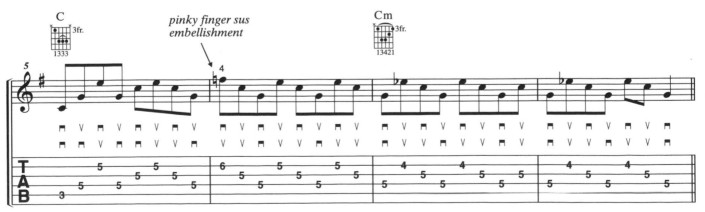

Also note how O'Brien embellishes the B and C chords (in the intro only) by adding his pinky on the 2nd string, one fret higher than his barred ring finger. This briefly creates a sus chord, but it moves by so quickly that it's not notated in the chord frames (and could be overlooked easily).

Guitarist Jonny Greenwood thickens up the chorus by doubling O'Brien's distorted power chords. He then brings the chorus to a climax by tremolo picking a rising octave pattern. Tremolo picking is essentially a very quick picking technique: simply move your hand up and down as quickly as you can (without any discomfort). The diagonal lines *≠* above each note in the notation and TAB indicate which notes you should tremolo pick.

Make sure to dampen the note between each set of octaves, or else the open 4th string will ring through. Fret the lower note with your index finger and the higher note with your ring finger, then roll that index finger downward until it dampens the 4th string. (For a tip on how to play the scratch rhythms in Gtr. 2's part, see the performance notes for "Life in the Fast Lane" on page 107.)

 **FUN FACT**

The members of Radiohead were all teenagers when they met in 1985 at an all-boys school. They'd meet on Fridays to play music, so they called themselves "On a Friday." They cut their teeth in an Oxford pub called Jericho Tavern—the same place where their future managers, Chris Hufford and Bryce Edge, noticed them.

 GUITAR GODS

RADIOHEAD was formed in Abingdon, England, in 1985 with a three-guitar lineup of Thom Yorke, Ed O'Brien, and Jonny Greenwood. "Creep" was the first single from their 1993 debut, *Pablo Honey*. Next came *The Bends* in 1995, and by 1997's *OK Computer*, Radiohead had become one of the biggest rock bands in the world.

Creep

Words and Music by
THOMAS YORKE, JONATHAN GREENWOOD,
PHILIP SELWAY, COLIN GREENWOOD,
EDWARD O'BRIEN, ALBERT HAMMOND
and MIKE HAZELWOOD

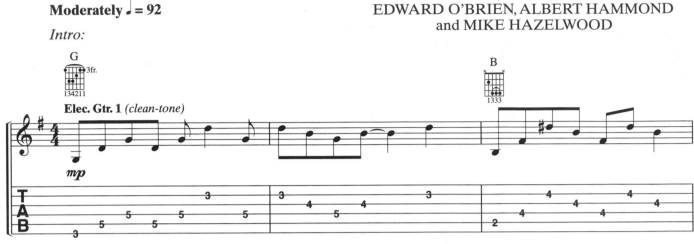

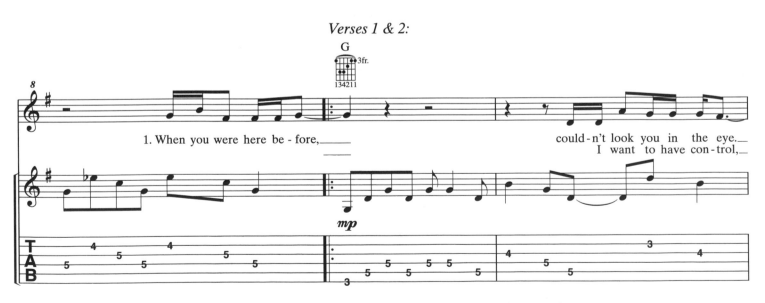

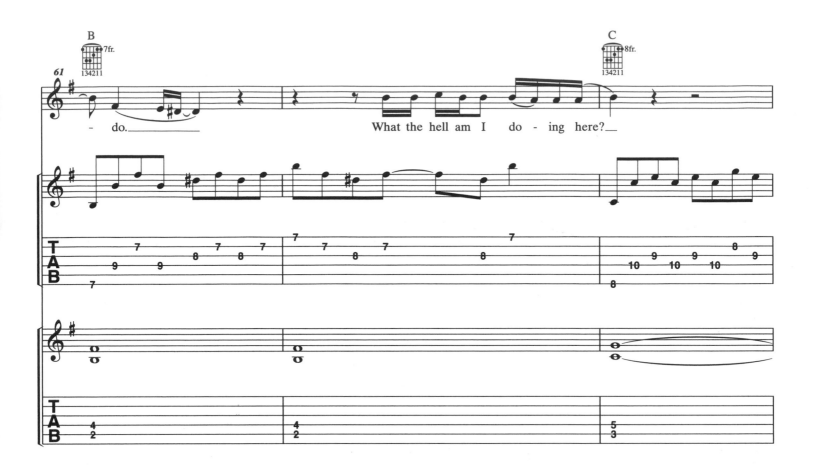

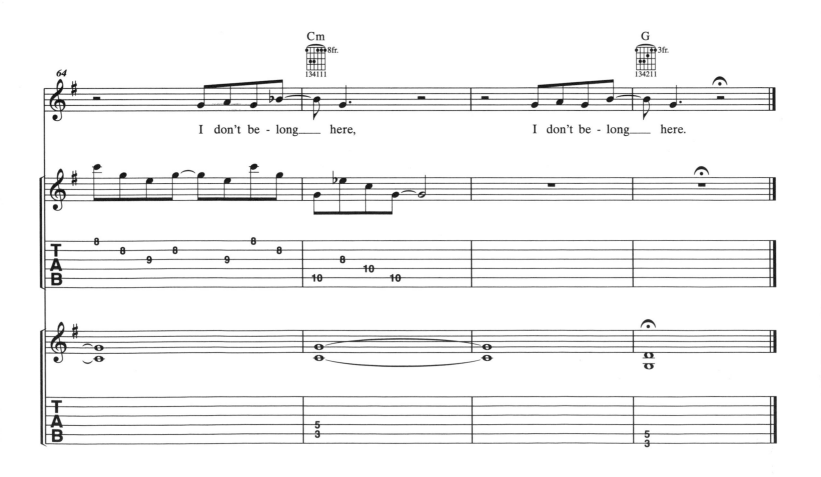

Gimme Some Lovin'

Key Thoughts

"Gimme Some Lovin' " by The Spencer Davis Group prominently showcases 18-year-old Steve Winwood's powerhouse vocal talents and his aggressive Hammond B-3 organ riffing. In this transcription, the signature organ part is arranged for guitar. Because there are only a few chords, the song may at first appear easy, but as with most blues-based music, the apparent simplicity of the transcription is deceptive. Listen to the original recording and try to infuse your performance with the same groove, energy, and dynamics.

Take Note

The intro is a driving *octave* G figure. For the organ riff, if you're playing a guitar without easy access to the upper register, you can transpose the notes down one octave by subtracting 12 from each TAB number.

DEFINITION

An **octave** is the interval between two notes with the same letter name. The frequencies of the notes are in multiples of two. For example, the A of the open 5th string has a frequency of 220 Hz (Hertz), which means it vibrates 220 times per second. The note A an octave above the open A string (the 2nd fret of the 3rd string) has a frequency of 440 Hz; 2 x 220 = 440.

The verse piano figure is played with the following two-measure strum pattern:

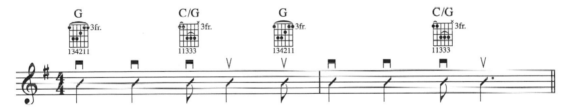

GUITAR GODS

Even at the height of the '60s British Invasion, guitarist **SPENCER DAVIS** and lead singer Steve Winwood had trouble getting both their music and the band into the U.S. Their first hit, 1965's "Keep On Running," was a smashing success in the U.K., but barely made the top 100 in America. The group finally won favor in the U.S. with "I'm a Man" and their hottest seller "Gimme Some Lovin'," which peaked at No. 7 on the U.S. charts. Despite such success, The Spencer Davis Group never performed in the United States. Winwood left the group to form Traffic in 1967 and later played with Eric Clapton in Blind Faith. A talented multi-instrumentalist (keyboards, guitar, bass, and mandolin), Winwood subsequently produced other acts, scored huge solo hits in the '80s, and recently teamed-up again with Eric Clapton for a series of sold-out and critically acclaimed concerts.

Gimme Some Lovin'

Words and Music by
STEVE WINWOOD, MUFF WINWOOD
and SPENCER DAVIS

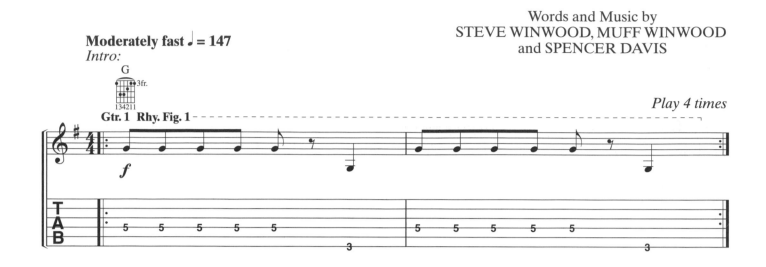

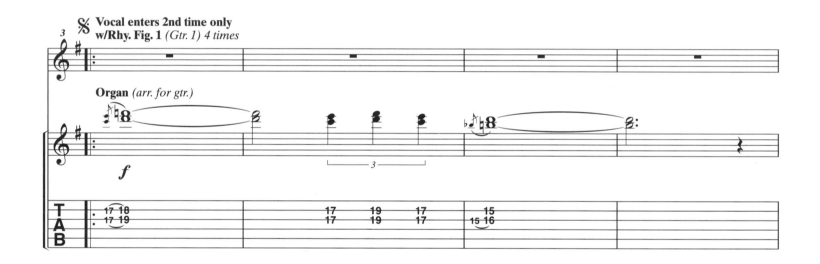

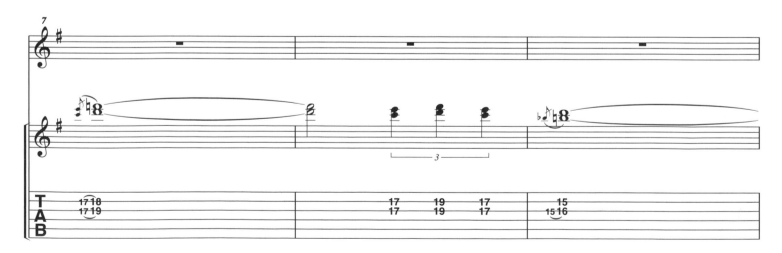

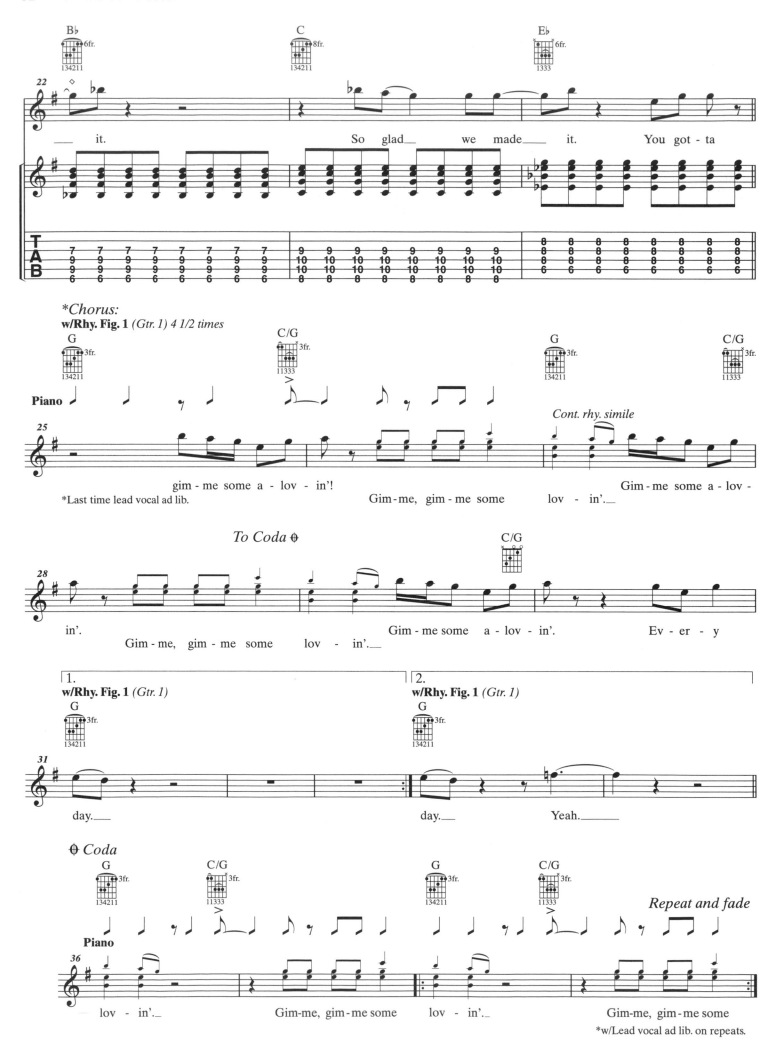

Hotel California

The Eagles' chart-topping masterpiece features music by guitarist Don Felder and lyrics by Don Henley and Glenn Frey. The song depicts a nightmarish scenario resulting from the hedonistic excesses of many affluent Americans in the late '70s— "You can check out anytime you like but you can never leave."

Note that Acous. Gtr. 1 (12-string) is capoed at the 7th fret and all other guitars are played without a capo, hence the two different sets of chord names. The chord symbols in italics above the frames throughout the music are for the 12-string acoustic guitar, and the chord names beneath the frames are for the other guitars (those frames are listed under the song title).

In the song's introduction, the 12-string guitar begins with a series of *arpeggios.* Hold your fretting fingers in the shape of the chord, and don't obsess about picking the notes exactly as transcribed. If you happen to strike a note that's not notated in the staff, you'll be hitting a chord tone, so it will sound all right. Play along with the provided recordings, and don't forget that you can slow them down with the TNT software and gradually work up to the right tempo.

DEFINITION

An **arpeggio** is a chord played one note after another, not all at once. Other famous rock songs that begin with guitar arpeggios include "Stairway to Heaven" and "The House of the Rising Sun."

In the chorus, Acous. Gtr. 1 opens with a Mexican-style strummed rhythm. If you're using a capo at the 7th fret, be sure to play the frames with the chord names in italics.

The guitar solo is not really easy to play, but it is very melodic. It's likely that you can already sing most of it, so you're halfway there. Even if you don't attempt the solo, use the play-along CD or get a friend to come over so you can try the harmonized arpeggios played by Elec. Gtrs. 3 & 4 in the outro. This figure is such a simple, but effective, way to close out the song.

 FUN FACT

Numerous interpretations of the hidden meaning in "Hotel California" have developed over the years. Some speculate that the song is about Satan and worship of the occult, and others think it's about an insane asylum. There's also the theory that it's about an inn run by cannibals, or that it depicts a descent into addiction. The fact is, it's simply a reflection of the real-world dangers faced by musicians caught up in the heady lifestyle of a rock star.

GUITAR GODS

EAGLES formed in 1971 with Bernie Leadon and Glenn Frey on guitar. By 1976, when "Hotel California" was recorded, Leadon had been replaced by Don Felder, and former James Gang leader Joe Walsh was brought onboard as a third guitarist. On the recording, Felder and Walsh exchange lead licks in one of the most famous guitar duets in history.

64

Hotel California

Bm   F#7   A   E   G   D   Em

Chord frames reflecting concert key (for uncapoed gtr.)

Moderately slow ♩ = 74

Intro:

Words and Music by
DON HENLEY, GLENN FREY
and DON FELDER

*Acous. Gtr. 1 w/capo VII, transposed to E minor.
  Chord frames and TAB numbers relative to capo.
  All other guitars w/o capo.
  Chord frames w/italic names above represent capoed gtr.
  Non-italic chord names under frames represent concert key.
  Chord frames reflecting concert key appear under song title.

Am
B7
Em
F♯7
There were voic-es down the cor - ri - dor,_ I thought I heard them_ say
Wake you up in the mid-dle of the night just to hear them_ say.
*Elec. Gtr. 2 (w/light dist.)
mf
Chorus:
*Composite arrangement. Simile on repeat.
C
G
G
D
Acous. Gtr. 1
Cont. rhy. simile
Wel - come_ to the Ho - tel Cal - i - for - nia, such a
Wel - come_ to the Ho - tel Cal - i - for - nia, such a
B7
F♯7
Em
Bm
love - ly place,_ such a love - ly face._
love - ly place,_ such a love - ly face._ They're
(Such a love - ly place._)
C
G
G
D
Plent-y of room_ at the Ho - tel Cal - i - for - nia. An - y
liv-ing it up___ at the Ho - tel Cal - i - for - nia. What a

"Re - lax," said the night - man, "We are pro - grammed to re - ceive."

You can check out an - y - time you like but you can nev - er leave.

Elec. Gtr. 3 *(w/light dist.)*

Guitar Solo:
w/Rhy. Figs. 1 *(Acous. Gtr. 1)* **& 1A** *(Elec. Gtr. 1) both 3 times, simile*

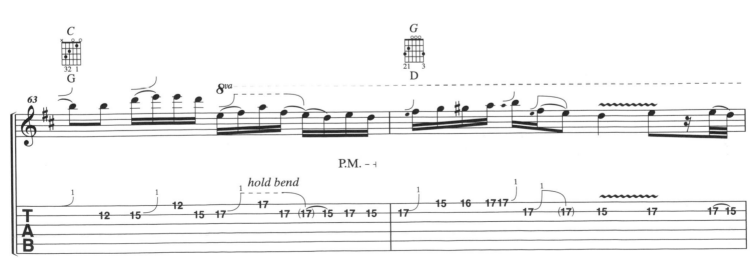

Outro:

w/Rhy. Figs. 1 *(Acous. Gtr. 1)* **& 1A** *(Elec. Gtr. 1) both simile*

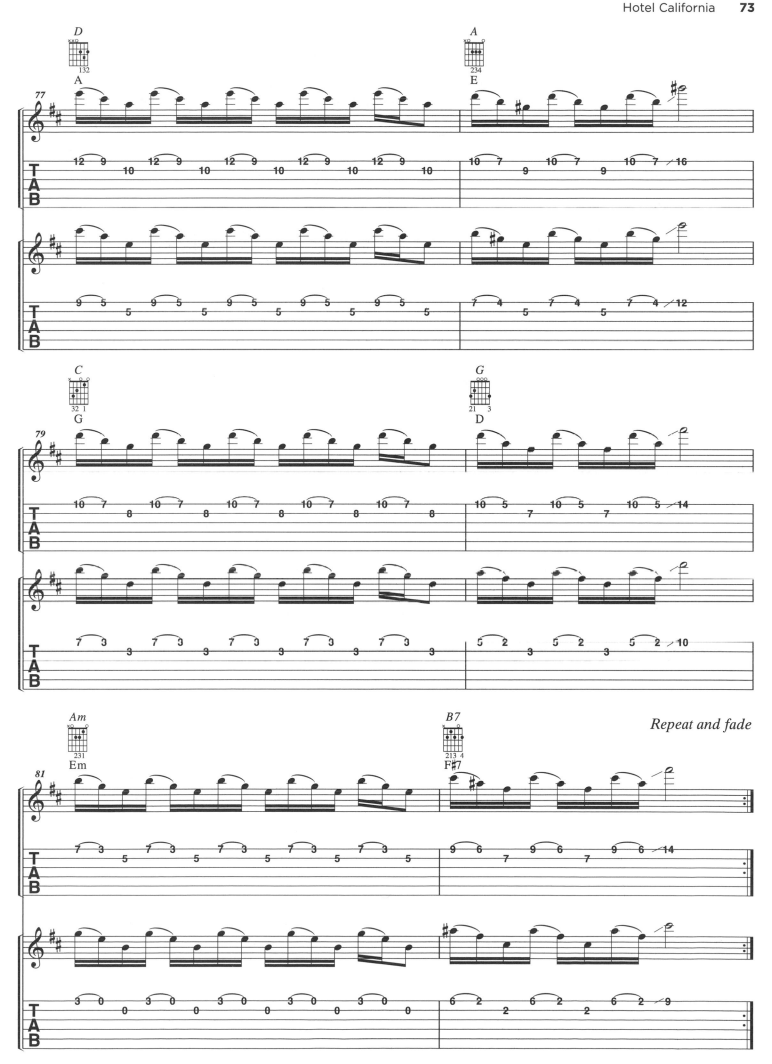

How You Remind Me

Key Thoughts

Canadian band Nickelback achieved commercial nirvana in 2001 with the pop/grunge blend of "How You Remind Me." The band's distinct style has led to a remarkable string of successes in the model established by this song.

Take Note

This song is in *Drop D tuning*. Drop D is identical to standard tuning, except the 6th string is tuned down a whole step from E to D.

In the verse, note the similarity between the chord frames for Csus2 and Fsus(9), and between B♭sus2 and E♭sus(9). The chords of each pair are actually the same, but with a shift of the bass note from the 5th string to the 6th string. When playing the 1st measure, hold your 1st-finger barre at the 3rd fret and your 3rd and 4th fingers at the 5th fret for Csus2. At the change to Fsus(9), simply move your index finger up from the 5th string to the 6th string. The change from B♭sus2 to E♭sus(9) is done the same way, but at the 1st fret.

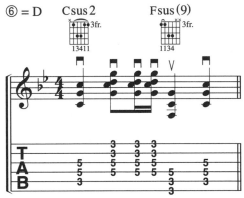

To emulate the strumming style in the verse that you hear on the recording, emphasize the bass strings of each chord on the first beat and try to strike the higher strings on the following beat. On the straighter eighth-note rhythm of the chorus, strike all the strings evenly with down-strokes, as shown below.

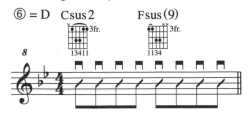

 ☆ **FUN FACT** ☆

The band's name is derived from the five cents change that bass player Mike Kroeger's brother often had to give customers in his job at a coffee shop, where he would say, "Here's your nickel back."

How You Remind Me

Lyrics by
CHAD KROEGER
Music by
NICKELBACK

Verse 2:
It's not like you didn't know that.
I said I love you and I swear I still do.
And it must have been so bad.
'Cause livin' with me must have damn near killed you.
(To Chorus:)

Go Your Own Way

Key Thoughts

Fleetwood Mac was one of the most successful bands of the '70s, and *Rumours* found them at the peak of their popularity. To help create a splash, the band released their first single, "Go Your Own Way," before the album's release. One of the top-selling records of all time, *Rumours* received the the Grammy for Album of the Year in 1978.

Take Note

The electric guitar drives "Go Your Own Way" with accented chord punches mixed with bass notes—all subtly controlled by careful *palm muting*. To palm-mute these notes, lay the fleshy outside edge of your picking hand across the strings at the bridge as you pick the strings. Practice applying pressure in varying degrees; the more pressure you use, the greater the string-dampening effect. This technique naturally mutes the bass strings more than the higher strings, allowing the chord punches to ring through.

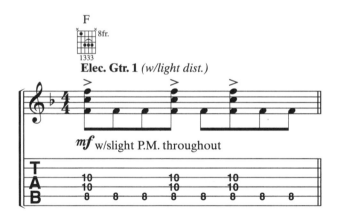

TIP

Lindsey Buckingham doesn't play with a pick, but, instead, uses his fingers to create a variety of sounds. For strumming, he'll either put his index finger and thumb together to emulate a pick, or he'll fling the backs of his fingers into the strings like a banjo player does when "frailing." He even employs this frailing-type strumming while playing single-note leads—sometimes using just one or two fingers to make the strings sound. While you can try these techniques out yourself, you don't *need* to play with your fingers to sound like Buckingham; if you're more comfortable playing with a pick, that will work fine.

Guitarist Lindsey Buckingham layers a 12-string acoustic guitar into the mix to fill out the rhythm. If you don't have a 12-string, don't worry; you can still pull it off. Make sure to add a capo to the 3rd fret for this part. Throughout the song, chord shapes for the acoustic guitar are italicized, while chord symbols that denote the concert pitch (the notes and chords you're actually playing, regardless of the chord's shape) are shown in parentheses. Note how Buckingham embellishes the D chord shape by lifting his middle finger off of the high E string, momentarily creating a Dsus2 chord. These embellishments move by so quickly that this chord symbol isn't shown:

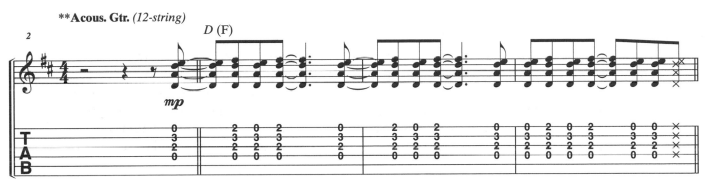

**Acous. Gtr. w/capo III. TAB numbers relative to capo.

☆ **FUN FACT** ☆

When Fleetwood Mac holed up in Sausalito, California, to record *Rumours* at the legendary Record Plant Studios, the group was wrestling with inner turmoil. Nearly every member of the band was splitting up—with *another* member of the band. In fact, Buckingham penned "Go Your Own Way" about his split with Stevie Nicks.

 **GUITAR GODS**

Well before their pop heyday, **FLEETWOOD MAC** started out in 1967 as a blues band, featuring guitarist Peter Green. After several lineup changes, the catalyst to pop stardom was the addition of Stevie Nicks and Lindsey Buckingham, who came as a package (they'd been previously working as the duo Buckingham Nicks). This meant the group now had three prodigious pop songwriters (Nicks, Buckingham, and Christine McVie), with Buckingham proving to be an ace producer, as well.

Go Your Own Way

Capo III → D A G Bm

Frames for Acous. Gtr. w/capo III.

Words and Music by
LINDSEY BUCKINGHAM

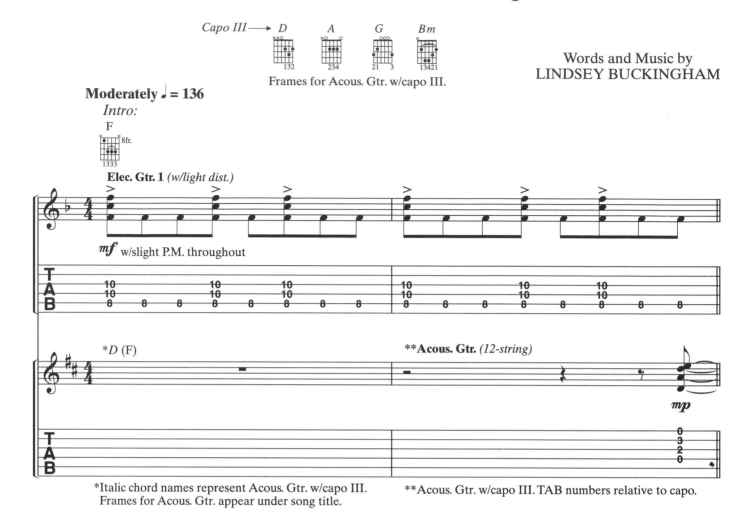

*Italic chord names represent Acous. Gtr. w/capo III.
Frames for Acous. Gtr. appear under song title.

**Acous. Gtr. w/capo III. TAB numbers relative to capo.

You can go___ your own___ way,_____ go___ your own___ way. ___ your own___ way.

Guitar Solo:

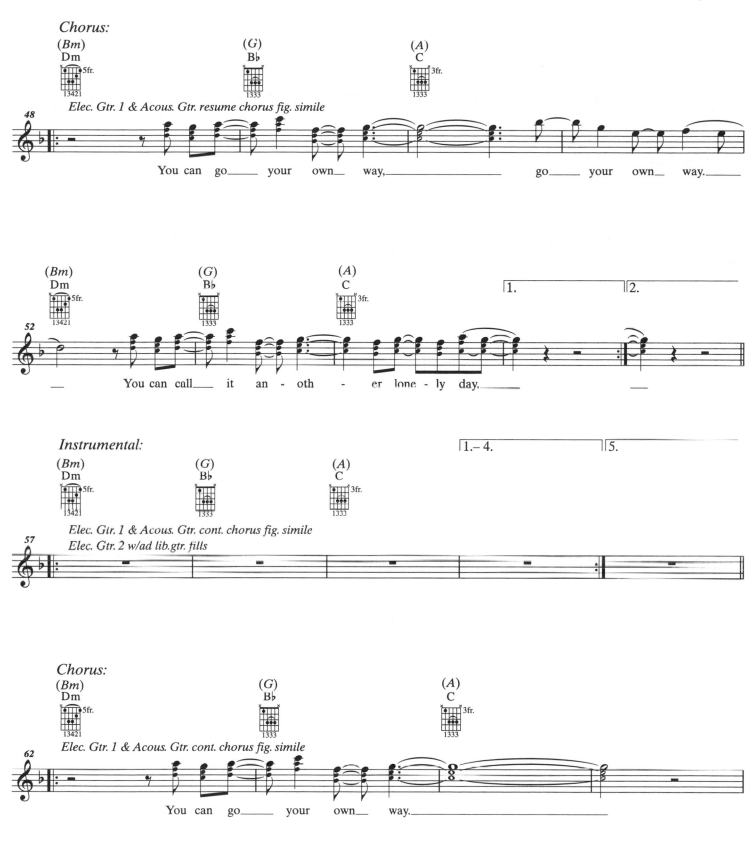

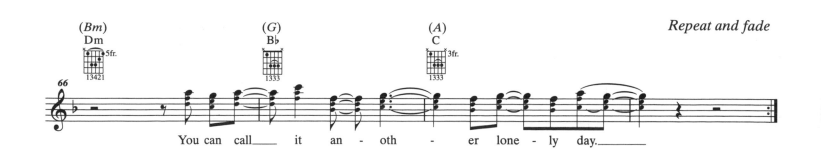

Immigrant Song

"Immigrant Song" kicked off *Led Zeppelin III*, and was also released as the album's only single. Paired with the hard-to-find B-side "Hey Hey What Can I Do," the track climbed to No. 16 on *Billboard*'s Hot 100. Using imagery from Norse mythology and Viking conquests, the song inspired countless heavy metal bands to incorporate similar themes into their music.

Guitarist Jimmy Page starts "Immigrant Song" with an octave riff that provides a perfect backdrop to Robert Plant's screaming wails. This riff is easy to play—just rock between your index finger on the 6th string and your ring finger on the 4th string, as shown below. Make sure to accent the first note of each beat, as shown by the > symbols. The words "simile throughout" in the second measure of the transcription indicate that you should continue with these accents throughout the song.

Intro:

When you reach the A chord in the verse, note the fingering—a barred index finger across strings 2–4. This fingering allows you to move more quickly between chords, and it's a staple trick of rock guitarists. (Fretting the chord like this makes it difficult to sound the high open E string, but you won't miss it that much.)

DEFINITION

A **tritone** is an interval of six half steps, called an augmented 4th or a diminished 5th, which splits an octave into two equal parts. The tritone is such a discordant interval that it's been called the "devil's tone." Within "Immigrant Song," you'll hear this in measure 36, when the chord jumps directly from F♯m to C9.

Several times within the song, Page jumps to a C chord—a discordant *tritone* interval away from the song's tonic ("home") chord of F♯m. In measure 24, over one of these C chords, Page plays a lick using the C major pentatonic scale. Lead licks are often built from scales in the song's key signature—in this case, F♯m—but the notes of the F♯ minor scale clash with the notes in a C chord, so that's why Page skillfully creates his lick from the C major pentatonic scale instead.

Page's C Major Pentatonic Lick   C Major Pentatonic Scale

FUN FACT

Led Zeppelin songs have been notoriously hard to license, and they rarely appear in movies or commercials. So when Jack Black wanted to use "Immigrant Song" in the movie *School of Rock*, he made a promotional video—complete with thousands of screaming fans in the background—in which he pleaded with the members of Led Zeppelin to let him use the song. The ploy worked, spurring Jack Black to say, "If you really want something, you might have to get down on your knees… with 1,000 people behind you screaming."

Immigrant Song

Moderately ♩ = 113

Words and Music by
JIMMY PAGE and ROBERT PLANT

Paralyzer

Canadian rockers Finger Eleven emerged in 1998 with their heavy debut record, *Tip*. Over the next decade, the band gradually modified their sound by adding in other stylistic elements. By the time they released *Them vs. You vs. Me* in 2007, they were sandwiching disco-like grooves, acoustic guitars, and tambourines between the heavy riffs, creating an eclectic—but cohesive—sound. "Paralyzer," the leadoff track on *Them vs. You vs. Me*, uses shades of funk and disco to drive the groove, adding a well-placed metal lick and powerful vocals to keep things rockin'. The track climbed Canadian and U.S. charts, and helped the record secure a Juno Award for Rock Album of the Year.

On the recording, guitarist James Black plays the main riff using notes all along one string (except for the low open E string). Start with your pinky on the 9th fret, your middle finger on the 7th fret, and your index finger on the 5th fret. Then, just slide down one fret to grab the 4th fret note with your index finger (bar 1, below). Since this riff is all along one string, you can play it in several places, and Black often plays it along the 5th string during live performances (bar 2, below). As you move to lower strings, you have to move up the neck, which makes the stretches easier because the frets are closer together. Black took advantage of this on the recording by playing the riff all along the 6th string—way up at the 19th fret (bar 3, below).

Play the licks be hind the verse in measures 11–12 by barring your index finger across the 3rd and 4th strings at the 12th fret. Then use your ring finger to grab the notes on the 14th fret. In measures 13–14, employ a similar technique—this time barring your index finger across the 2nd and 3rd strings, using your middle finger on the 12th fret.

 **FUN FACT**

The inspiration for "Paralyzer" came during a photo shoot. To keep themselves from looking too awkward on film, the band started jamming, and came up with the song's riff. The opening Em chord was a lucky accident. It came from a later part of the song, but the band accidentally left it in when shuffling sections around in the studio to see how things sounded in a different order. They liked the way it sounded so much that they kept it, overdubbing the vocal swell and drums.

Paralyzer

Music and Lyrics by
SCOTT ANDERSON, SEAN ANDERSON,
RICH BEDDOE, JAMES BLACK and RICK JACKETT

*Chords are implied throughout.

Chorus:

A5 · **G**

- es what your eyes can do,____ you'll prob-'bly move right_ through_ me on my way to_ you._

Outro:

Em · **A5**

— You'll prob - 'bly move right_ through

G · **Em**

me on my way to_ you.___

A5 · **G** · **N.C.**

You'll prob - 'bly move right_ through me on my way to you.___

Know Your Enemy

Key Thoughts

It took Green Day five years to follow up 2003's hugely successful *American Idiot*, but their 2009 release, *21st Century Breakdown*, was worth the wait. By early 2010, the album had topped the charts in the U.S., Europe, and the U.K.—a feat unmatched by any previous Green Day record. "Know Your Enemy" was the first single from *21st Century Breakdown*, and it was Green Day's first hit to top *Billboard*'s Rock Songs, Alternative Songs, and Mainstream Rock Tracks charts all at the same time.

Take Note

Guitarist Billie Joe Armstrong is a master at using barre chords and quick chord changes to craft melodic rhythm parts—a hallmark of punk guitar songs—and "Know Your Enemy" is a great example of this. Rhythm figure 1 (shown below) is the foundation of much of the song. This part is shown in slash notation, and each diagonal line represents a chord strum instead of a single note. As you strum through, make sure to dampen the strings for the "x" strums indicating *scratch rhythm*. (For more on scratch rhythm, see the performance notes for "Life in the Fast Lane" on page 107.) At the end of the third measure below, notice the standard notehead; this tells you to play a single note, not a strum. The string number is circled below the notehead, and the fret number is shown above (in this case, play the open string).

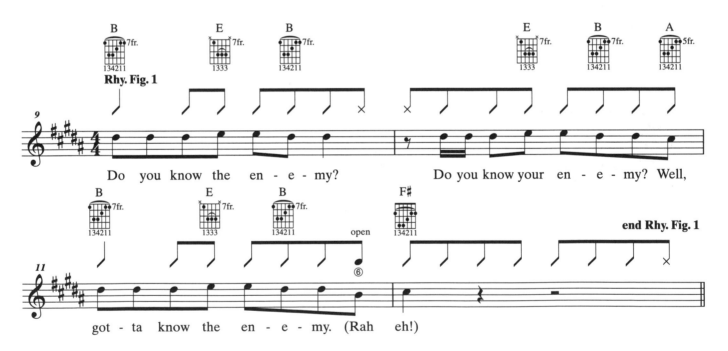

To play th[is] [...]ee your index finger[...] [...]et, assigning one finger per subsequent fret (that means you[...] [...] 12th, 13th, and 14th frets, respectively). From this position, y[...] and—that is, until you reach the bridge section, part of wh[ich] [...] down so that your index finger is on the 9th fret, and assign [...] [f]rets. The single note on the 8th fret might make you want t[o] [...] aligned over the 9th–12th frets and reach down with your [...] [wi]ll be easier to grab.

⭐ **FUN FACT** ⭐

Green Day's *American Idiot* and *21st Century Breakdown* were both concept albums. *American Idiot* was adapted into a musical and had such a successful debut at the Berkeley Repertory Theatre in California that it moved on to Broadway in early 2010.

GUITAR GODS

Singer/guitarist Billie Joe Armstrong and bassist Mike Dirnt formed their first band, Sweet Children, in 1987 when they were both just 15 years old. John Kiffmeyer (also known as Al Sobrante) joined them on drums a year later, and by the time they released their debut record in 1989, they had changed their name to **GREEN DAY**. When Kiffmeyer left for college in 1990, drummer Tré Cool filled in—eventually becoming Green Day's permanent drummer. The band enjoyed underground success until their third record, *Dookie*, made them international stars in 1994, selling over 20 million records to date.

Know Your Enemy

Lyrics by BILLIE JOE
Music by GREEN DAY

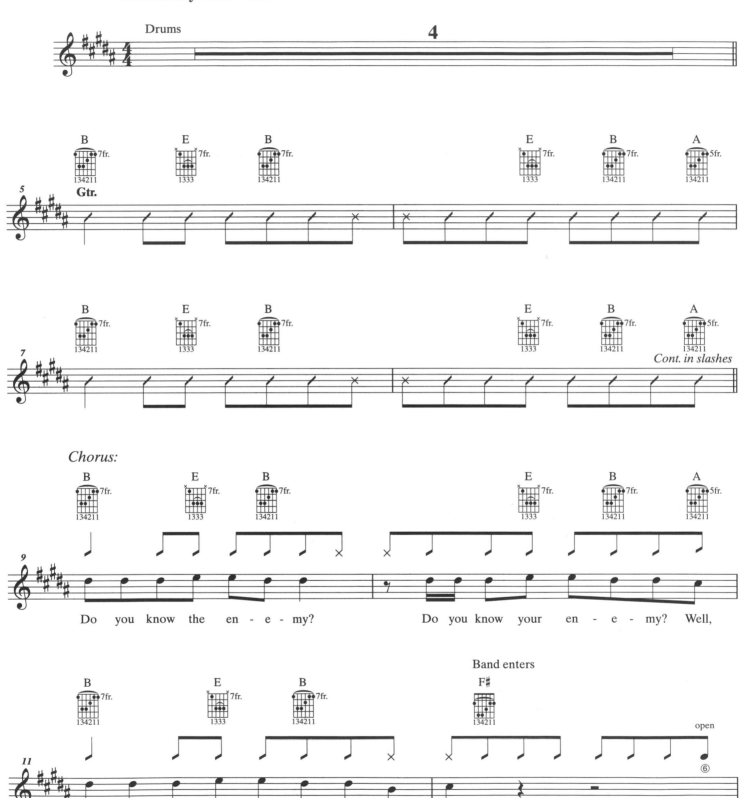

To play the guitar solo, use your index finger at the 11th fret, assigning one finger per subsequent fret (that means your middle, ring, and pinky fingers will be on the 12th, 13th, and 14th frets, respectively). From this position, you can access every note without moving your hand—that is, until you reach the bridge section, part of which is shown below. At this point, slide your hand down so that your index finger is on the 9th fret, and assign your other fingers to the 10th, 11th, and 12th frets. The single note on the 8th fret might make you want to move out of position, but if you keep your hand aligned over the 9th–12th frets and reach down with your index finger for that note, the rest of the lick will be easier to grab.

☆ **FUN FACT** ☆

Green Day's *American Idiot* and *21st Century Breakdown* were both concept albums. *American Idiot* was adapted into a musical and had such a successful debut at the Berkeley Repertory Theatre in California that it moved on to Broadway in early 2010.

GUITAR GODS

Singer/guitarist Billie Joe Armstrong and bassist Mike Dirnt formed their first band, Sweet Children, in 1987 when they were both just 15 years old. John Kiffmeyer (also known as Al Sobrante) joined them on drums a year later, and by the time they released their debut record in 1989, they had changed their name to **GREEN DAY**. When Kiffmeyer left for college in 1990, drummer Tré Cool filled in—eventually becoming Green Day's permanent drummer. The band enjoyed underground success until their third record, *Dookie*, made them international stars in 1994, selling over 20 million records to date.

Know Your Enemy

Lyrics by BILLIE JOE
Music by GREEN DAY

B   E   B   F#

27

volt a - gainst the hon - or to o - bey. (Oh eh, oh eh.)

% *Verses 2 & 3:*
w/Rhy. Fig. 1 *(Gtr.) 2 times*

B   E   B   E   B   E   B

29

O - ver-throw the ef - fi - gy,   the vast ma - jor - i - ty, well, burn - ing down the fore-man of con -

F#   B   E   B   E   B   A

trol. (Oh eh, oh eh.)   Si - lence is the en - e - my,   a - gainst your ur - gen - cy, so

B   E   B   F#   *To Coda* ⊕

35

ral - ly up the de - mons of your soul. (Oh eh, oh eh.)

Chorus:
w/Rhy. Fig. 1 *(Gtr.) 2 times*

B   E   B   E   B   A

37

Do you know the en - e - my?   Do you know your en - e - my? Well,

B   E   B   F#

39

got - ta know the en - e - my. (Rah eh!)

B   E   B   E   B   A

41

Do you know the en - e - my?   Do you know your en - e - my? Well,

got - ta   know   the   en - e - my.   (Rah   eh!)   The   in -

Bridge 1:

sur - gen - cy   will   rise____   when   the   blood's   been   sac - ri - ficed.

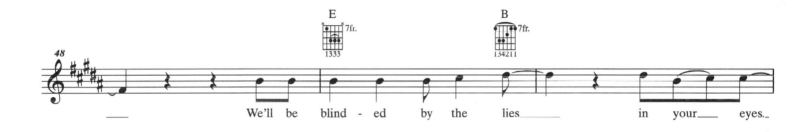

____   We'll   be   blind - ed   by   the   lies____   in   your____   eyes._

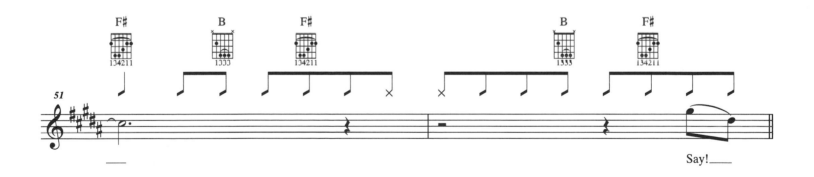

____   Say!____

Guitar Solo:
w/Rhy. Fig. 1 *(Gtr.) 2 times*

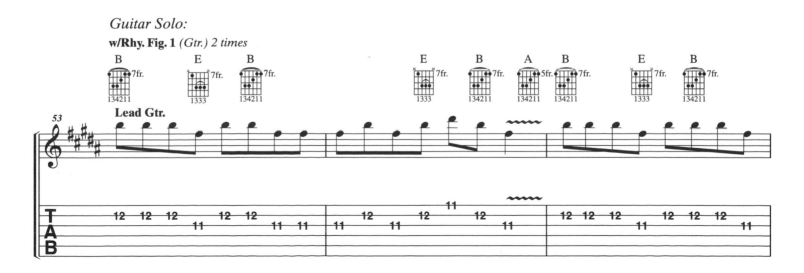

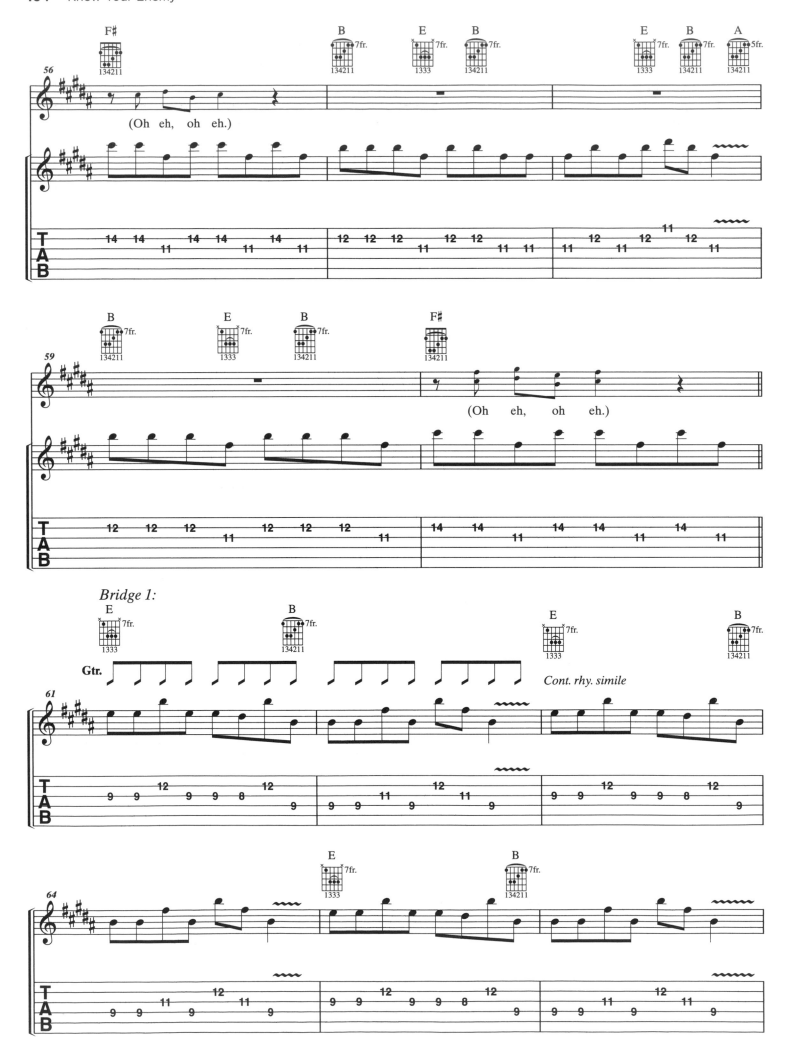

Life in the Fast Lane

Key Thoughts

The Eagles reportedly spent eight months in the studio working on their fifth release, *Hotel California*. The hard work paid off, as the record became one of the top-20 selling records of all-time in the U.S. This was the Eagles' first outing with guitarist Joe Walsh, who replaced Bernie Leadon and injected more of a rock sound into the group's songs via his harder-edged electric guitar riffs and solos.

Take Note

Guitarist Joe Walsh puts his stamp on "Life in the Fast Lane" from the downbeat by opening the song with a driving electric-guitar riff that lasts four measures. Walsh builds this riff from a two-measure phrase, but notice how he doubles it (and also makes the riff more interesting) by shifting the second half of it an eighth note over as he repeats the riff. Look at the example below to see how this works; the second two measures are identical to the first two, except that measure 4 slides the notes from measure 2 an eighth note earlier—the lick now starts on the last eighth note of measure 3, instead of on the downbeat of measure 4.

FUN FACT

On the original vinyl release of *Hotel California*, the words "V.O.L.: is five piece live" are inscribed on side 2, on the inside of the run-out groove. This somewhat cryptic quote means that the song "Victim of Love" was recorded live in one take as a five-piece band.

The E9 chord frame above the verse represents the overall sound, and strumming through this single chord shape will work fine as an alternative to the funk rhythm line beneath it in notation and TAB. But Walsh's part doesn't use this complete shape, and it's easier to play the riff if you don't fret the whole chord. Instead, barre across the top three strings with your index finger at the 7th fret, then use your ring finger to barre across the 9th fret on the "&" of beat 2. (You'll have to slide up to barre the 12th fret with your ring finger on the "&" of beat 3.) Play the two-string shapes on the 4th and 5th strings in the same manner: use your barred index finger for the 9th fret notes, then slide up to grab the 14th fret barre with your ring finger, leaving your index finger in place for the 12th fret barre. The move from the 12th fret barre to a hammer-on at the 13th fret is a great way of highlighting the most important notes in a seventh (or ninth) chord—the 3rd and flat 7th—and it's a common move in funk and blues.

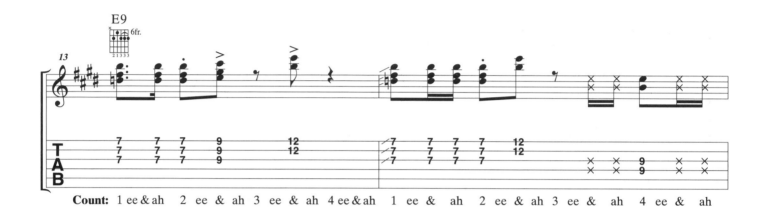

If you have trouble with the funky rhythms, slow down and count along using sixteenth-note subdivisions (as shown above). Remember, if you use the included CDs in your computer, you'll be able to access the slow-down and loop features for this song.

TIP

The "x" noteheads in the notation and TAB are **scratch rhythms**. To play scratch rhythm, lift your fingers off the chord just enough to dampen the strings, then strum through with your picking hand to produce a percussive "chukka" sound.

Life in the Fast Lane

Moderate rock ♩ = 110
Intro:

Words and Music by
DON HENLEY, GLENN FREY
and JOE WALSH

Verse 1:

hard-head-ed man,_ he was bru-tal-ly hand-some, and she was ter-mi-nal-ly pret-ty.

She held him up and he held her for ran-som in the heart_

_____ of the cold,_ cold____ cit-y. He had a nas-ty rep-u-ta-tion as a

Layla

With passionate lyrics inspired by an ancient Persian love poem, music composed to express unrequited love for a best friend's wife, a fiery riff borrowed from a blues song, a vocal sung with heart-wrenching desperation, and a piano coda created by a tragically mentally ill drummer, "Layla" boasts a pedigree like no other song. With all its disparate elements, it was destined to become Eric Clapton's signature song, and is a standard by any measure.

Eric Clapton initially conceived "Layla" as a slow blues shuffle, but Derek & the Dominos decided the song was better served at a moderate tempo.

The intro is in the key of D minor. The signature riff was added at the suggestion of guest guitarist Duane Allman. It's a sped-up version of the vocal line from Albert King's "As the Years Go Passing By." The riff is first established in a lower octave and in open position, combined with some double stop power chords (root & 5th) that also serve as the chorus chord progression.

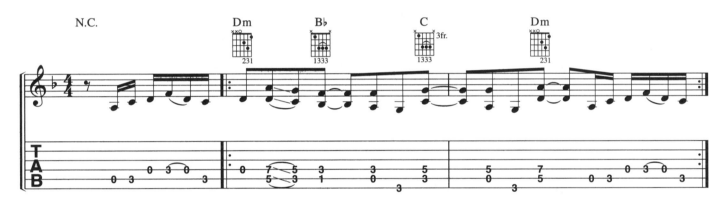

At measure 4, a second guitar introduces the riff two octaves higher, at the 10th-fret position. Notice that there is a slight variation at the end of each alternating phrase. On the first pass (measure 5), the 1st-string F at the 13th fret is bent up a whole step to G. On the next pass (measure 7), the G at the 15th fret is bent up a whole step to A. This change will require you to shift your left hand momentarily out of the 10th-fret position. For these notes, support your little finger with the other fingers of your left hand to help push up the string.

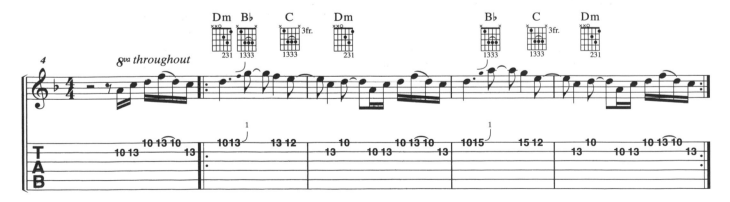

The verse modulates to the key of C♯ minor (or E major) and is characterized by a slightly funky rhythm that wraps up with a series of ii–V–I sequences. The rhythm pattern may look complicated, but as with most new things, if you break it down and take your time, you'll find it's actually not difficult at all. Try to strum it using the down-strokes and up-strokes shown in the example below. The two muted sixteenth notes at the end of the measure give your left hand a chance to reposition for the next chord.

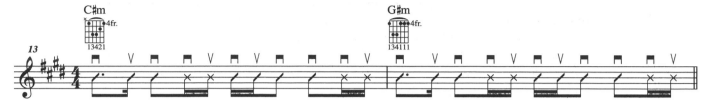

The final chorus (in the key of D minor) ends on a suspended C major chord that establishes a new key for the piano coda. The song's beautiful outro was composed (and performed on the piano on the original recording) by Jim Gordon, the drummer for Derek & the Dominos. You can either play the melody, which is transcribed in the notation, or you can strum the chords. The chord progression features an unexpected yet lovely twist in the form of a B♭9(♭5) chord, shown at right.

$B\flat9(\flat5)$

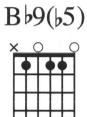

TIP

When music modulates to another key, it almost always means a change in the key signature and a new group of sharps or flats. If you're reading notation and don't notice the change, you'll find yourself playing a lot of odd-sounding notes.

FUN FACT

The sunburst guitar featured on "Layla" (as well as in the photograph on the album's back cover) is a 1956 Fender Stratocaster purchased by Clapton in 1967. Known as "Brownie," the guitar was sold at an auction in 1999, raising $450,000 for Clapton's Crossroads Centre for the treatment of drug and alcohol addiction.

GUITAR GODS

Weary of the intense adulation heaped on him from his tenure with the Bluesbreakers (when graffiti appeared around London proclaiming "Clapton Is God"), his period in the spotlight in Cream, and the quickly aborted supergroup Blind Faith, Eric Clapton chose to retreat to relative anonymity in 1969 as a sideman in the American rock/soul band Delaney & Bonnie & Friends. While touring with Delaney & Bonnie, Clapton forsook the bombast of his trademark setup (a Gibson humbucker-equipped guitar plugged into a pair of cranked Marshall stacks) for a more subtle combination of a Fender Stratocaster and smaller Fender amplifiers. In Delaney and Bonnie's band, Eric found future **DEREK & THE DOMINOS** members Carl Radle, Jim Gordon, and Bobby Whitlock. The Dominos' only album was recorded in Miami in 1970 with guest guitarist Duane Allman and failed to make much of an immediate commercial or critical impact. Most likely due to drug abuse and frustration, the band fell apart in 1971 before they could complete a second album. It wasn't until 1972 that "Layla" became a top 10 hit, elevating itself and its attendant album to undeniable classic status.

Layla

Words and Music by
ERIC CLAPTON and JIM GORDON

Moderately ♩ = 117

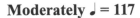

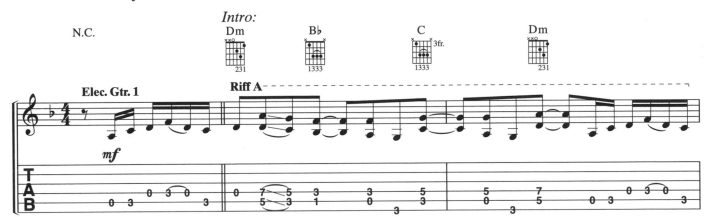

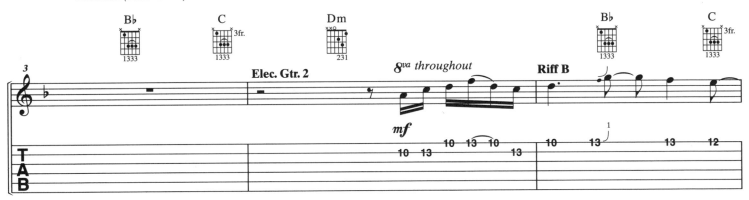

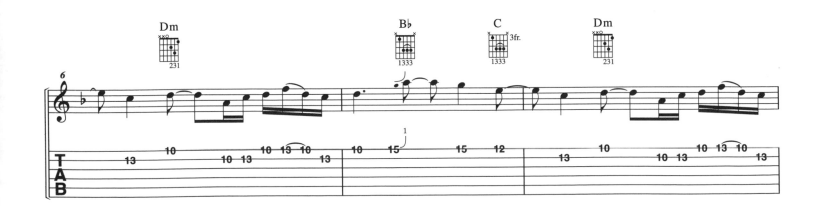

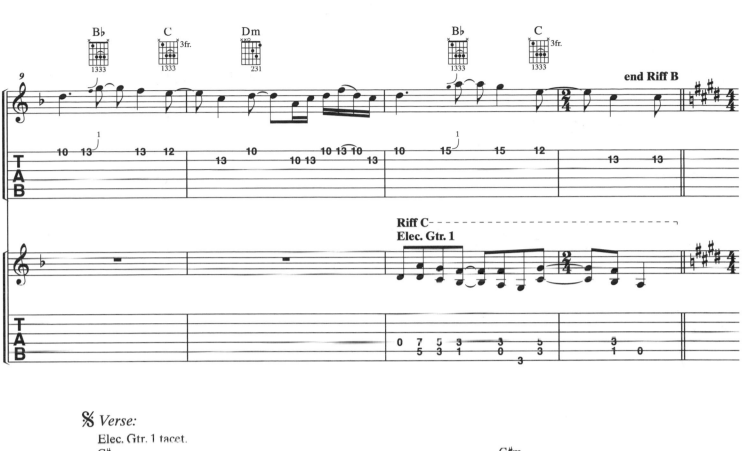

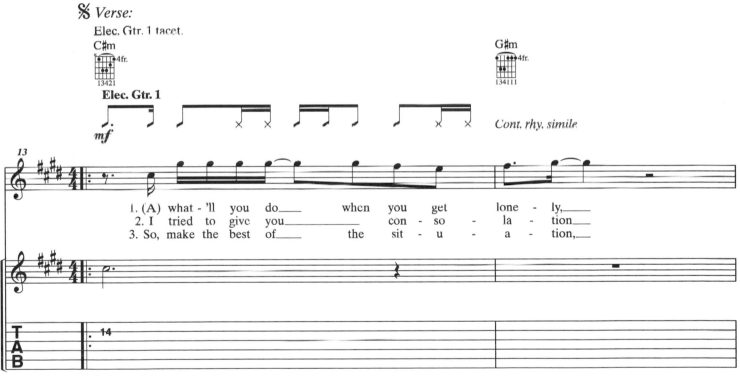

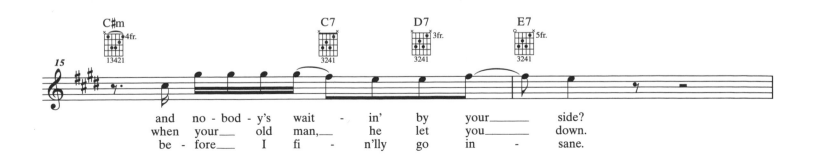

Coda I

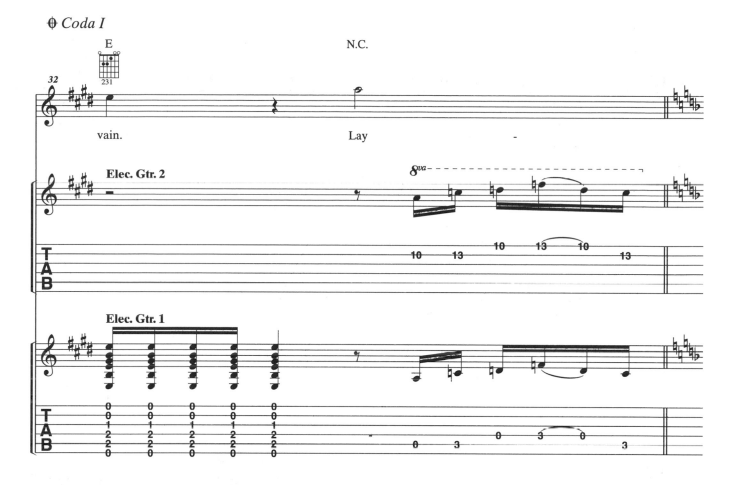

vain.   Lay -

Chorus:
w/Riff A *(Elec. Gtr. 1) 4 times*
w/Riff B *(Elec. Gtr. 2) 1st 4 meas. only, 2 times*

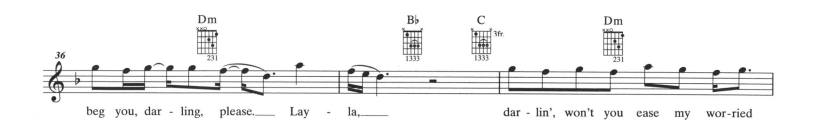

la,_____   you got me on__ my knees.__ Lay - la,_____   I

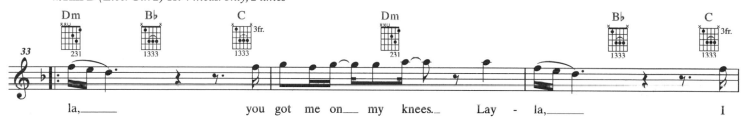

beg you, dar - ling, please.__ Lay - la,_____   dar - lin', won't you ease my wor-ried

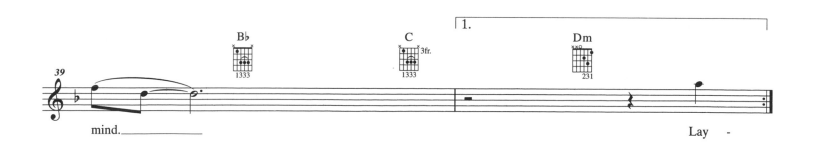

mind._____   Lay -

Long Train Runnin'

Key Thoughts

The guitar part to "Long Train Runnin'" is quintessential Doobie Brothers. This is the song that had every young guitarist in the '70s trying to learn how to play that "killer strum"—the fast, fluid, funky constant sixteenth-note groove that drives the entire band.

Take Note

Like so many other songs, the signature guitar part of "Long Train Runnin'" is the intro. To play this rhythm groove, you first need to *listen to the music.* (Whoops! Wrong Doobie Brothers song, but still very true.) Sorry about the joke, but be sure to listen carefully to the original recording or the provided sound-alike so you know how this is supposed to sound. Music notation can only give you so much information, and the rest comes from listening.

The secret to playing this guitar part is to strum a constant stream of sixteenth notes combined with some muted percussive strums. A few well-placed hammer-ons create an inside melody within the constant strum. The intro rhythm figure is played with a barre at the 10th fret, striking all strings but the 6th string. Strum the notes at the 10th fret, and immediately hammer your 2nd and 3rd fingers down on the 11th and 12th frets to form the Gm7 chord. Then, the trick is to release the left hand's pressure on the chord while maintaining the constant sixteenth-note strum to create a strong percussive part. Reapply the pressure so that the chord is sounded as shown in the following example; the muted chords are shown with "x" noteheads. After you've played it for a bit, see the additional tips that follow.

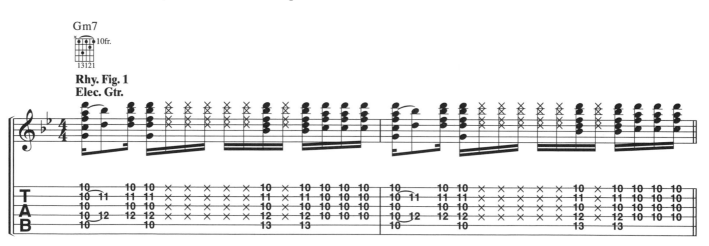

Here are some more tips for getting the correct feel:

- As you play the constant sixteenth-note strum pattern, be sure to strum from your wrist and keep a loose hold on the pick.

- Listen to the recording to hear the effect of the muted strums intermingled withthe full chords. Use your ear as a guide for when to mute the strings.

- Once you get the pattern under your fingers, close your eyes and listen to yourself play. Again, use your ear to guide you. Your hands will automatically begin to bring out the melodies and percussive parts by responding to your ear.

While the electric guitar plays the part shown in the preceding example, an acoustic guitar plays the fairly simple line shown below.

The electric and acoustic guitars continue throughout the song. An interesting "crossing" of the parts occurs on the change to the Cm7 chord, which is first shown at bar 9. At this point, the acoustic guitar plays Rhy. Fig. 2A, which sounds essentially like a continuation of what the electric guitar plays over the Gm7 chord. Meanwhile, the electric guitar plays a classic funk-style groove on Cm7 to Cm13. It is very common for guitarists to combine the Gm7 groove of the electric guitar with the Cm7 groove of the acoustic guitar. Learn all the parts and see what you prefer.

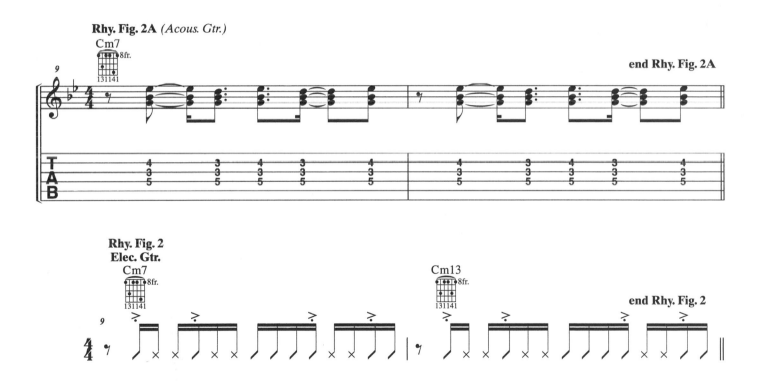

 **FUN FACT**

This song, and most of the rest of The Doobie Brothers catalog, was produced by Ted Templeman. Templeman was with the group Harpers Bizarre in the '60s. (Remember "Feelin' Groovy"?) In 1977, he brought a then-unknown group, Van Halen, to Warner Bros., and produced their first six albums. In the Van Halen song "Unchained," his is the voice that pleads, "Come on Dave, gimme a break," to which David Lee Roth replies, "One break, coming up!"

Long Train Runnin'

Words and Music by
TOM JOHNSTON

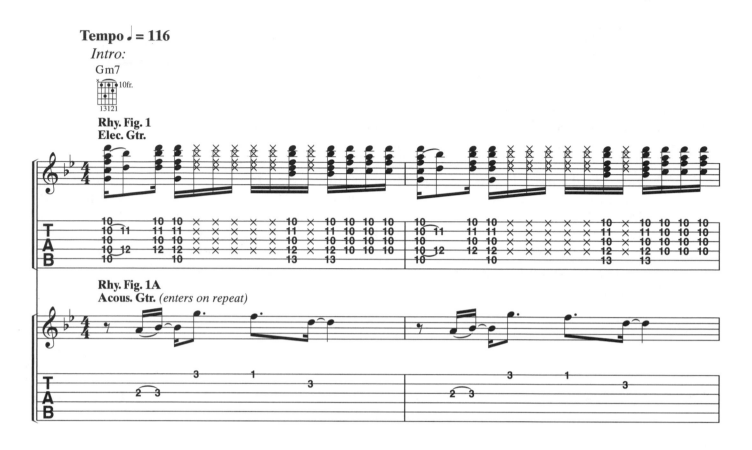

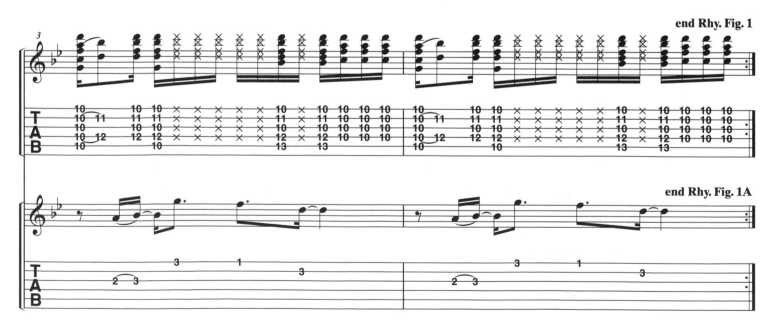

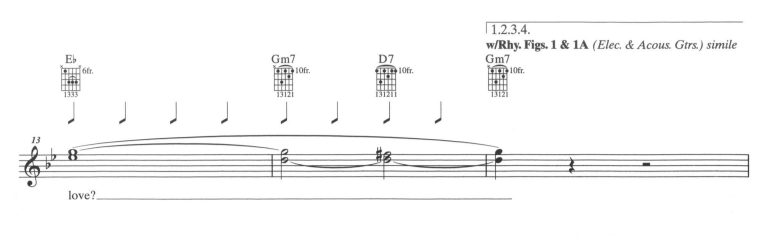

love?

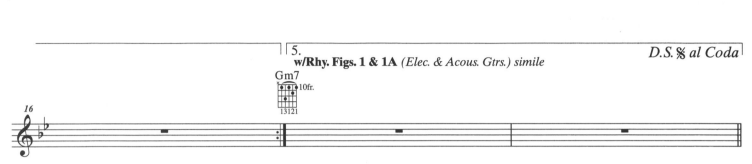

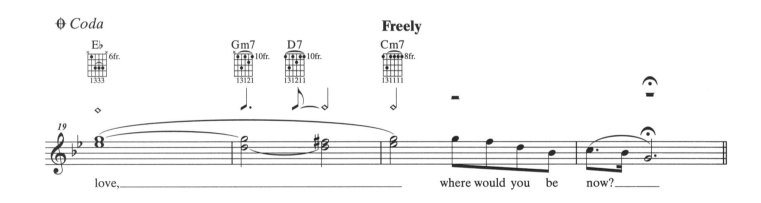

love,

where would you be now?

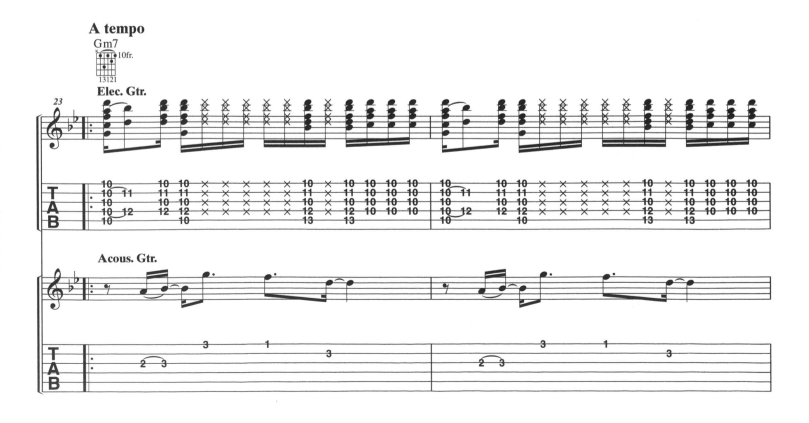

Repeat ad lib. and fade

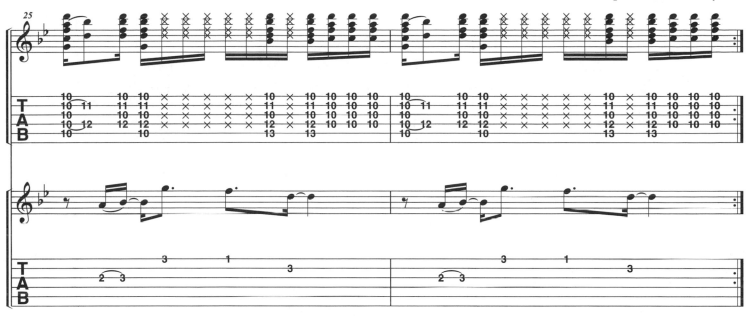

Verse 2:
You know I saw Miss Lucy,
Down along the tracks;
She lost her home and her family,
And she won't be comin' back.
Without love, where would you be right now,
Without love?

Verses 3 & 5:
Well, the Illinois Central
And the Southern Central freight,
Gotta keep on pushin', mama,
'Cause you know they're runnin' late.
Without love, where would you be right now,
Without love?
(1st time to Verse 4:)
(2nd time to Verse 6:)

Verse 4:
Instrumental Solo
(To Verse 5:)

Verse 6:
Where pistons keep on churnin'
And the wheels go 'round and 'round,
And the steel rails are cold and hard
For the miles that they go down.
Without love, where would you be right now,
Without love?
(To Coda)

Ramblin' Man

Brothers and Sisters was the first complete Allman Brothers Band album recorded after guitarist Duane Allman's death in a motorcycle accident. While Duane was irreplaceable, strong tracks like "Ramblin' Man" and "Jessica" prove that guitarist/singer Dickey Betts was more than capable of shouldering a heavy load. Betts influenced the band by bringing it slightly away from the blues and more squarely into Southern rock. "Ramblin' Man" hit No. 2 on *Billboard*'s Hot 100, and went on to become one of the band's most memorable and enduring singles. Other than Lynyrd Skynyrd's "Sweet Home Alabama," no other song embodies the Southern rock genre more than this one.

The rhythm guitar part to "Ramblin' Man" is made up entirely of barre chords. If your fingers get tired, you can always play open-position versions of these chords. If you do this, you'll have to mute the strings between strums with either hand to get the bouncy feeling on the record:

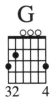 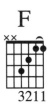   

Throughout the song, Dickey Betts plays leads taken primarily from the G major pentatonic scale—a scale commonly associated with the Southern rock sound. The major pentatonic gives Dickey that sweet, open country sound that he is known for.

Two-Octave G Major Pentatonic Scale

Betts rarely deviates from the G major pentatonic scale, but when he does—like in measures 4 and 52—he adds notes from the G major scale:

Two-Octave G Major Scale

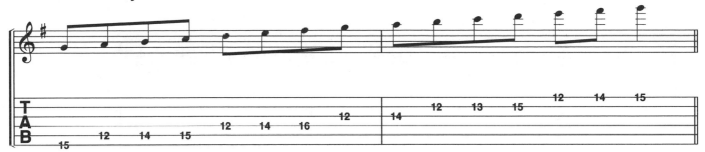

The only other note Betts adds to these scales is the B♭ (♭3rd) note in measures 55 and 66.

☆ **FUN FACT** ☆

The original *Brothers and Sisters* album cover featured Vaylor Trucks (the son of drummer Butch Trucks) on the front cover, and Brittany Oakley (the daughter of bassist Berry Oakley) on the back cover. Butch Trucks's nephew, Derek Trucks, is now a guitar god in his own right and considered one of the greatest blues slide guitarists in the world.

GUITAR GODS

Brothers Duane and Gregg Allman formed **THE ALLMAN BROTHERS BAND** in 1969 in Jacksonville, Florida. Added to Duane's guitar and Gregg's keyboards were Dickey Betts on guitar, Berry Oakley on bass, and Butch Trucks and Jai Johanny Johanson on drums. The band immediately established themselves and built up a following as a premiere jam band, kicking out fiery blues jams like their version of "Whipping Post" from the live recording *At Fillmore East*. While the group later became known for their radio-friendly Southern rock, in songs like "Blue Sky" and "Ramblin' Man," they never left the jam-band torch behind—especially at live shows.

Over the years, the band has had many accomplished guitarists—most notably Duane Allman and Dicky Betts, but also Warren Haynes and Derek Trucks.

Ramblin' Man

Words and Music by
DICKEY BETTS

Moderately fast ♩ = 182

Intro:

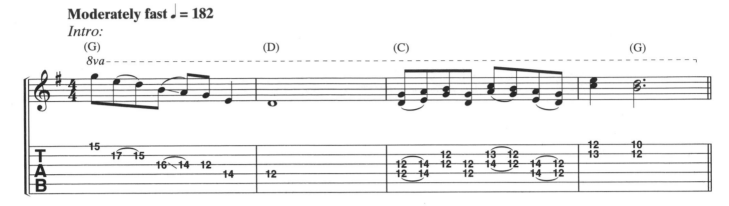

Chorus:

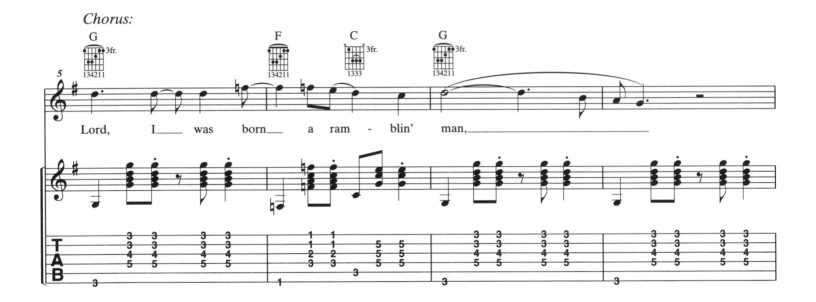

Lord, I___ was born___ a ram - blin' man,_____

Cont. rhy. simile

try'n' to make a liv - in' and do - in' the best I___ can.___ And

when it's time___ for leav - in', I hope you'll un - der - stand___

The Reason

Key Thoughts

Playing the main guitar riff from the verse of this song will do wonders for your pick technique. The riff is such an obvious good technical exercise that, like the riff to "Sweet Child O' Mine," it may have started life as a technical study.

Take Note

This riff has wide string skips. We suggest you use a pick because the riff will teach you tremendous pick control, but you have the option of using your fingers if that is easier. If you do use your fingers, use your thumb to play all the bottom notes and your middle finger to pluck the top melody. You could also use a "hybrid" pick and finger technique, in which your pick plays the bottom bass note and either your middle or ring finger plucks the top melody line.

Essentially, the riff consists of a bass note (always the root of the chord) that constantly alternates with a simple melody drawn from the chord shape. The riff moves from the E chord to the C#m, A, and B chords. Below are the fingerings for each pattern, isolated so you can practice them slowly. In these examples, the chord frame above the music shows the basic hand position required to play the riff, and the left hand fingers are given below the notes. In the song arrangement, the chord frames show you the strumming chords.

Here is the pattern for the E chord.

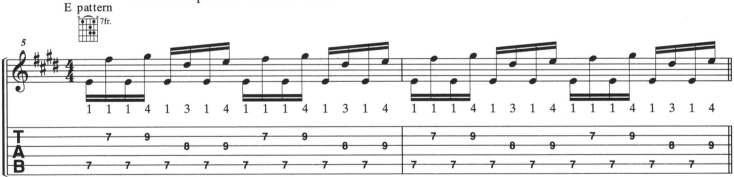

The next example is the pattern for the C#m chord. Notice that the fingering is basically parallel to the E chord pattern, just moved down to the 4th fret and altered to work over a minor chord instead of a major chord.

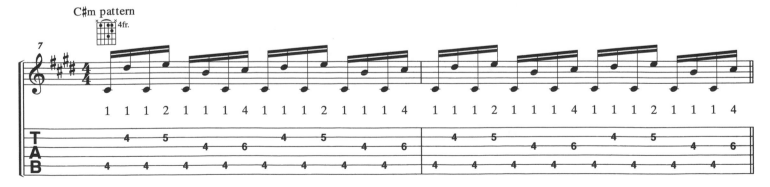

The A chord pattern is exactly the same as the pattern for C#m, only using an open A as the bass note instead of a C#.

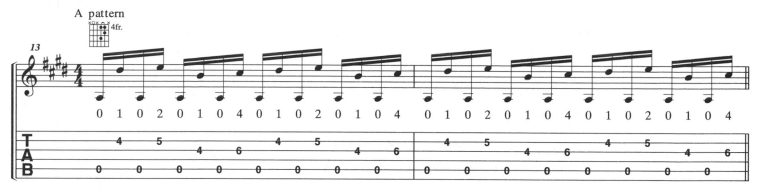

Here, the pattern slides down to the 2nd fret to work over the B chord.

GUITAR GODS

Playing an emotional, melodic brand of grunge-influenced rock, **HOOBASTANK** had one the biggest hits of 2004 with "The Reason." After the band's succession of radio and MTV hits including "Crawling in the Dark" and "Running Away," "The Reason" finally helped the band reach mainstream success. The Southern California-based quartet formed when singer Doug Robb met guitarist Dan Estrin at a battle-of-the-bands competition in high school. Soon after, they added bassist Markku Lappalainen and drummer Chris Hesse, and Hoobastank remains one the best young bands in rock today.

The Reason

Words and Music by
DANIEL ESTRIN and
DOUGLAS ROBB

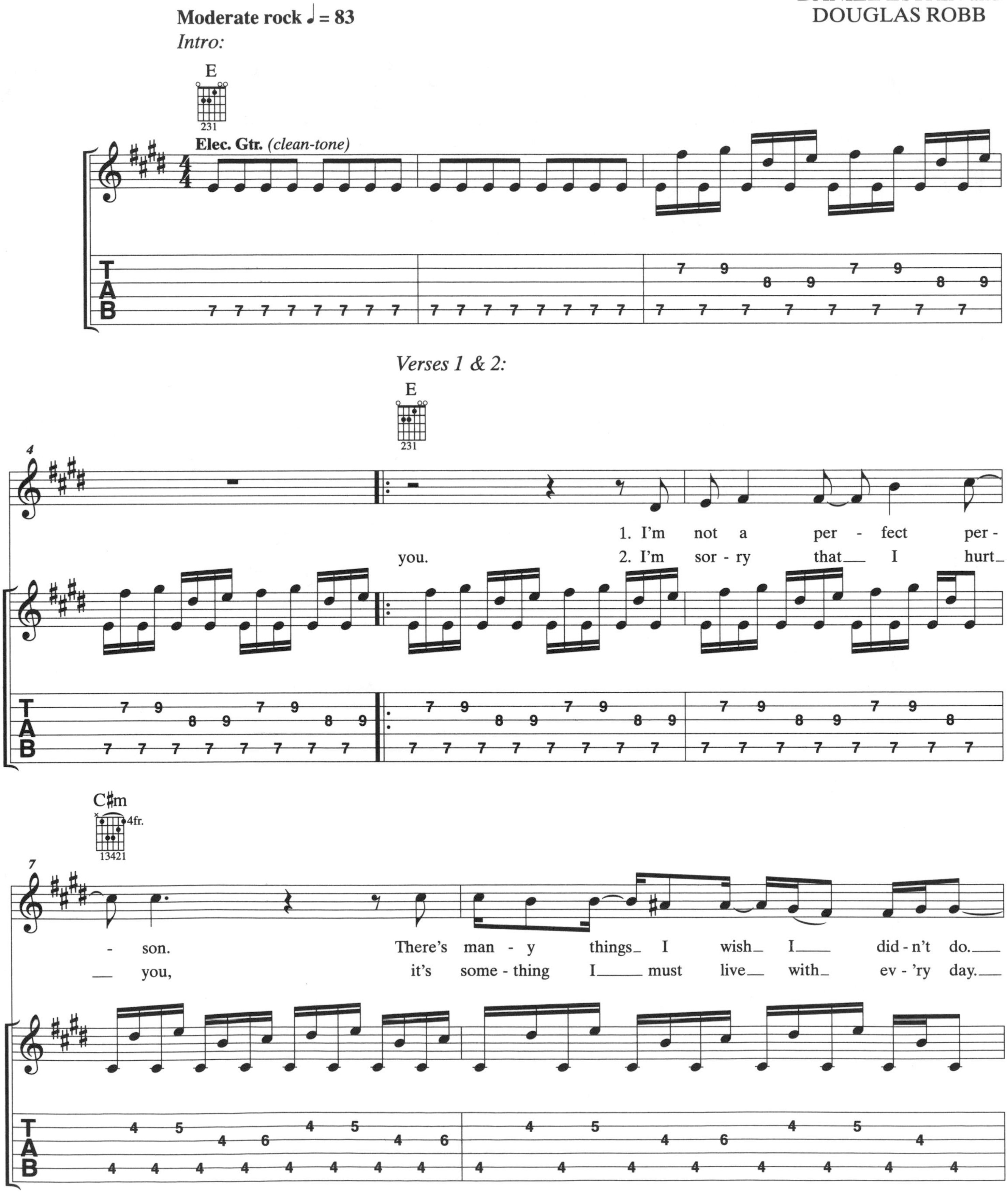

Moderate rock ♩ = 83
Intro:
E
231
Elec. Gtr. (clean-tone)
Verses 1 & 2:
E
231
1. I'm not a per - fect per -
you. 2. I'm sor - ry that I hurt
C♯m
4fr.
13421
- son. There's man - y things I wish I did - n't do.
you, it's some - thing I must live with ev - 'ry day.

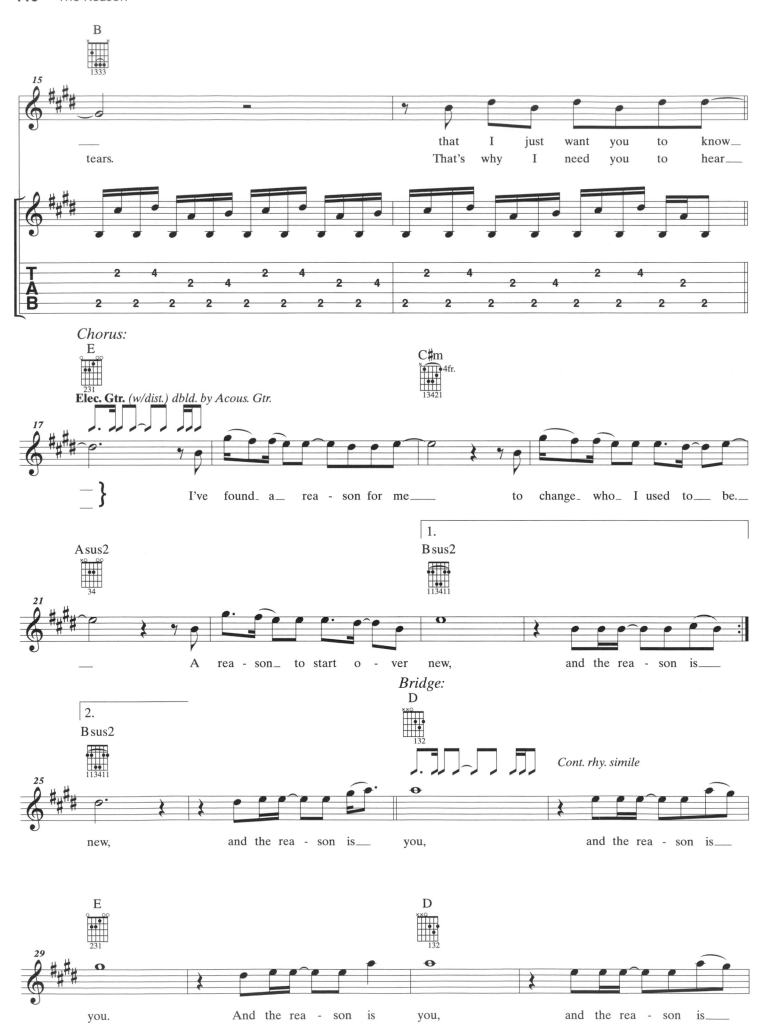

Smooth

Santana's 1999 release *Supernatural* saw the band collaborating with a variety of pop and rock stars on nearly every track. While most of these collaborations were fruitful, none came close to the success of the hit single "Smooth," featuring Rob Thomas. The track sat atop *Billboard*'s Hot 100 chart for so long that *Billboard* writer Fred Bronson ranked it the No. 1 song of the rock era in his book *Billboard's Hottest Hot 100 Hits*. Penned by Matchbox Twenty frontman Thomas and songwriter Itaal Shur, the song features Carlos Santana weaving his soulful guitar lines between Thomas's lead vocals. "Smooth" won two Grammys (Best Pop Collaboration with Vocals, and Record of the Year), *Supernatural* won two more (Album of the Year and Best Rock Album), and four other songs on the record won Grammys ("Maria Maria," "El Farol," "Put Your Lights On," and "The Calling") —a total of eight Grammys for one record.

Carlos Santana sculpts his singing guitar riffs by quickly shifting between two related minor scales: the *minor* (or *natural minor*) scale, and the *harmonic minor* scale (see below).

The harmonic minor scale is a minor scale with a raised 7th degree. This scale was created for *exactly* the type of situation we see in "Smooth." In minor keys, the V chord is minor. But dominant V chords resolve much more strongly than minor V chords do, so in minor key songs, the dominant V chord is often used in place of the minor V chord (E7 instead of Em). The dominant V chord has one note that's different from the minor V chord—the same note that corresponds to the 7th degree of the harmonic minor scale (the G♯ note in an A harmonic minor scale). So, in the case of "Smooth," the E7 uses the raised 7th degree of the A minor scale (G♯ instead of G).

As you can see, these scales share every note except for one—the G note in the minor scale becomes a G♯ in the harmonic minor scale.

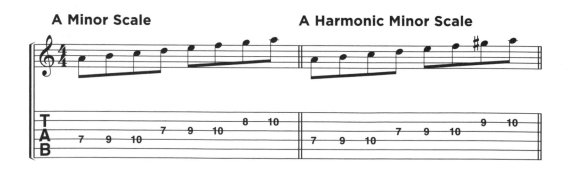

Why does Santana switch from natural minor to harmonic minor? It's because the E7 chord has a G♯ in it, and a G note would clash against that G♯. If you look carefully at the following lead line you'll see that Santana *only* uses the harmonic minor scale over the E7 chord, to match the G♯ note in the chord. Over every other chord, he uses notes from the A minor scale. This is the most common and important usage of the harmonic minor scale—not over the minor I chord (Am), but over the V7 chord (E7).

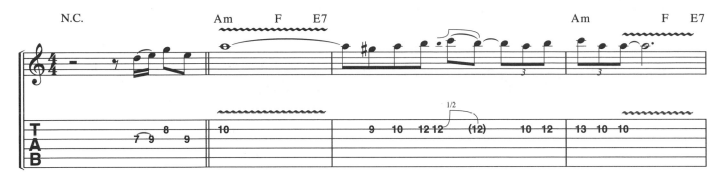

 TIP

Playing the guitar (and any instrument) goes beyond simply playing the notes, and Carlos Santana's guitar playing is a great example of this. As you listen to the recording, pay careful attention to how he manipulates his tone with judicious use of hammer-ons, pull-offs, slides, bends, and vibrato; much of Santana's tone is in his fingers. If you want to sound like Santana, practice these techniques until you can emulate the sound of the recording.

 **GUITAR GODS**

SANTANA emerged from San Francisco's psychedelic 1960s era behind the soulful, bluesy guitar playing of Carlos Santana. Santana's enormous success has made the band's sound the benchmark of many Latin-tinged rock acts. While the band has had many lineup changes over the years, their sound has remained distinct due to Carlos Santana's unique playing. (Neal Schon joined Santana as a teenager in 1971, playing guitar on three of the band's records before leaving with founding Santana keyboardist Gregg Rolie to form another hugely successful band—Journey.)

Smooth

Words and Music by
ITAAL SHUR and ROB THOMAS

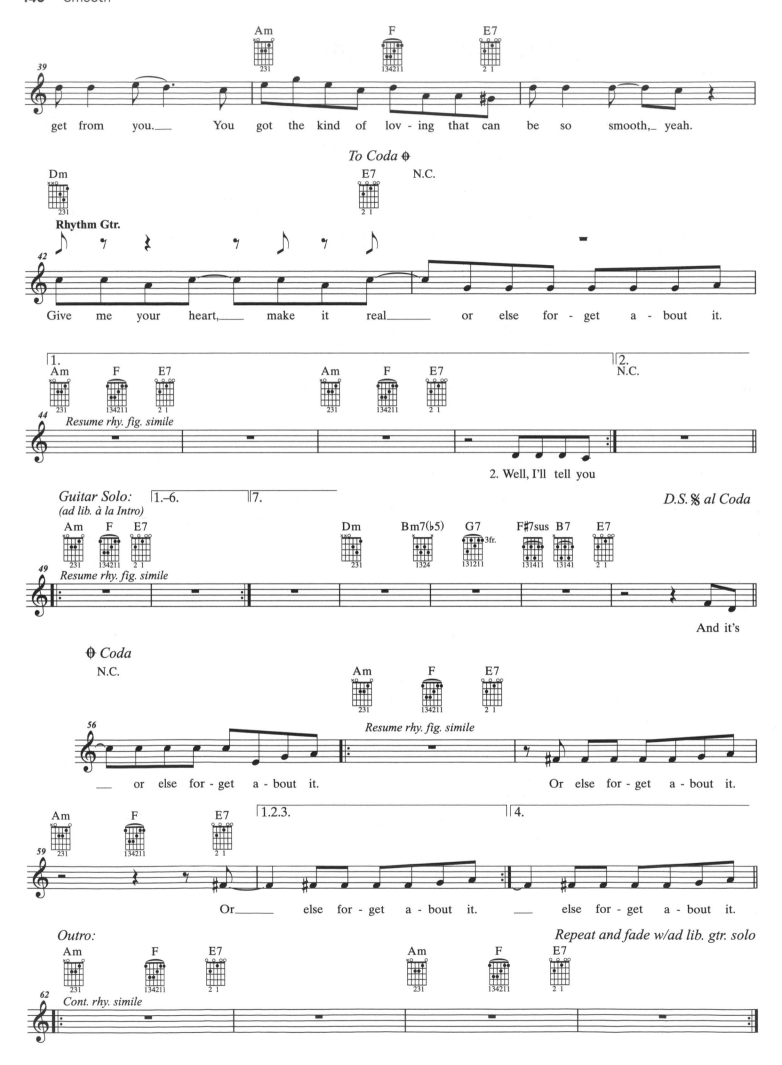

Stairway to Heaven

Key Thoughts

Arguably the most popular rock song of all time, "Stairway to Heaven" almost needs no introduction. An epic tune featuring what's often cited as the best guitar solo ever recorded, "Stairway to Heaven" is omnipresent on classic radio playlists and in the guitar-testing section of music stores. Included on Led Zeppelin's untitled fourth album, the song has reportedly been requested more than any other song on FM radio, even though it was never released as a single.

Take Note

The opening of "Stairway to Heaven" is played fingerstyle on an acoustic guitar. In general, play the down-stemmed notes with your thumb and the up-stemmed notes with your index, middle, and ring fingers. You can easily access all the notes in the first phrases with your those three fingers placed on the top three strings. Note that the thumb plays up-stemmed notes on the 5th string in measure 4:

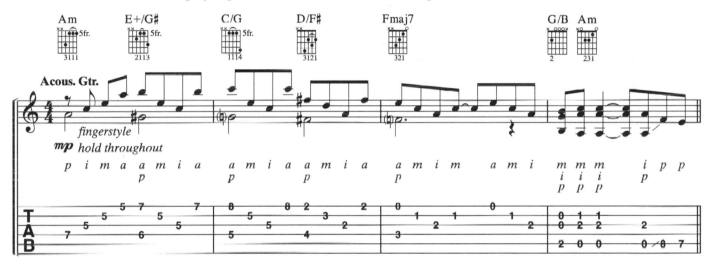

As the fingerpicking patterns spread across more strings, occasionally you'll need to move your fingers to skip a string or jump to a different three-string grouping, as seen in the following phrase from measures 9–12 of the song:

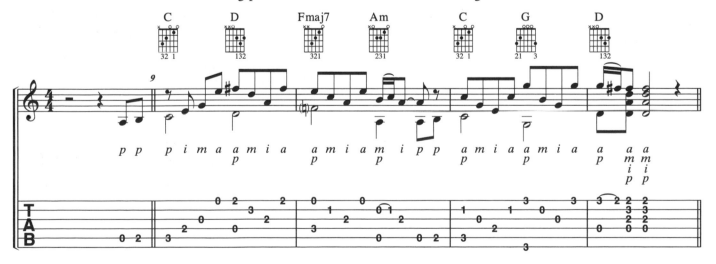

At measure 41, Page starts strumming chords. You can grab a pick for this section, or form your index finger and thumb into a pseudo-pick to play the rest of the song. The strummed interlude features easy-to-grab chords and embellishments at the nut for the first two measures, but jumps up for several tricky chord shapes in measures 43 and 44. Practice changing between the Am7 and Em/D *slash chords*, then practice the switch between Em/D and D. Notice that every chord after the Am7 in measure 43 is a three-note shape over the open D string, and that, after the D chord in measure 44, you simply slide the same shape down two frets and back up again.

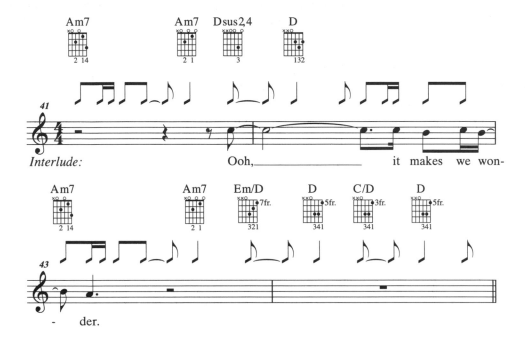

DEFINITION

Slash chords have a bass note that is not the *root note*. They are labeled with the chord name followed by the bass note, separated with a slash (hence the name). Slash chords are stated as the chord's name "over" the bass note; for instance, the C/G chord in "Stairway to Heaven" is called "C over G."

 **FUN FACT**

Before the Yardbirds and Led Zeppelin, Jimmy Page was a prolific session guitarist, and he played on many hits by other groups throughout the '60s. While the credits are somewhat contentious, and Page himself claims not to remember everything he contributed to, he reportedly played fuzz guitar on Donovan's "Mellow Yellow" and rhythm guitar on Them's rendition of "Baby Please Don't Go." He also reportedly played on The Kinks' debut record and even on The Who song "I Can't Explain."

Throughout Page's amazing guitar solo, he stays mostly within several positions of the minor pentatonic scale (see below). The position at the 5th fret has one variation that extends the scale up a note. To move to the upper extension, use your ring finger to slide from the 7th fret to the 9th fret where shown. Page occasionally adds an F note to the scale, which he gravitates toward every time the rhythm guitar plays an F chord. In measures 106 and 112, Page uses the first pattern but shifts it up an octave (12 frets).

A Minor Pentatonic Scale   **A Minor Pentatonic Scale with Extension**   **Added F Notes (for F Chord)**

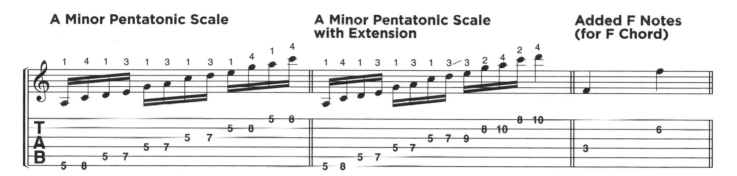

A Minor Pentatonic Scale with Extension   **Added F Notes (for F Chord)**

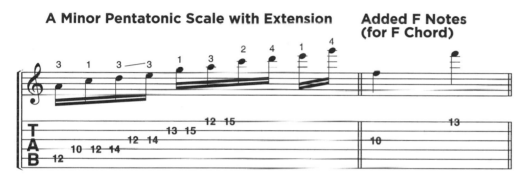

There are many bends in the solo, so make sure you back up your bending finger with another finger or two, or your fingers might get tired—especially on the 1½-step bends and the huge 2-step bend near the end of the solo. Use your ring finger for the bend at the end of measure 104. That way your pinky will be free to add the next note over the held bend.

At the end of the song (measures 132–141), Page plays a different set of bends—a series of rising *unison bends*. (For more on unison bends, see the lesson for "Cocaine.")

GUITAR GODS

The seeds for **LED ZEPPELIN** were sown in 1966, when guitarist Jimmy Page joined the Yardbirds (initially as their bass player before switching to guitar). As the group began falling apart in 1968, Page tried to recruit singer Terry Reid, who declined but suggested another talented young singer: Robert Plant. After Plant joined, he recommended John Bonham as the group's drummer. Now all they needed was a bass player, and Page tapped John Paul Jones; the two had crossed paths often as session players, and they enjoyed playing together. Initially performing as the New Yardbirds, the group quickly changed their name to Led Zeppelin to set themselves apart from the Yardbirds.

Stairway to Heaven

Words and Music by
JIMMY PAGE and ROBERT PLANT

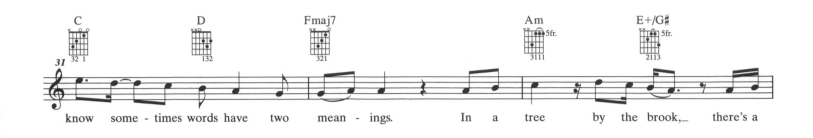

know some - times words have two mean - ings.   In a   tree   by the brook,___ there's a

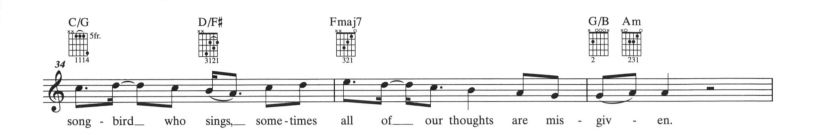

song - bird___ who sings,___ some - times all of___ our thoughts are mis - giv - en.

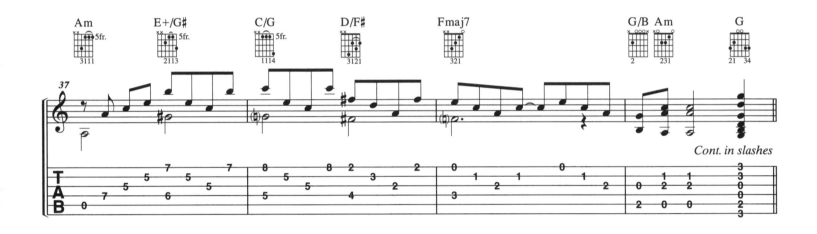

Cont. in slashes

Interlude:

Rhy. Fig. 1

Ooh,_____ it makes we won - der.

end Rhy. Fig. 1

Ooh,_____ it makes me won - der._____   2. There's a

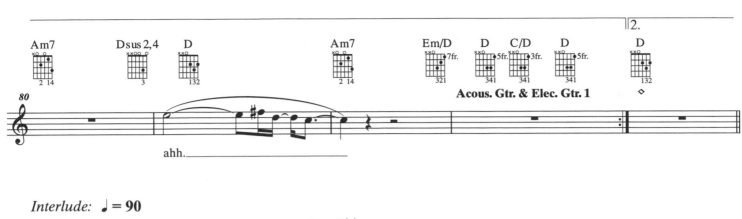

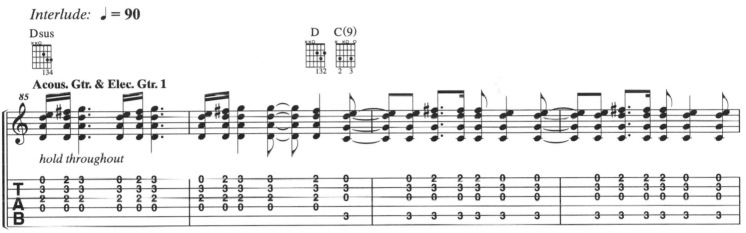

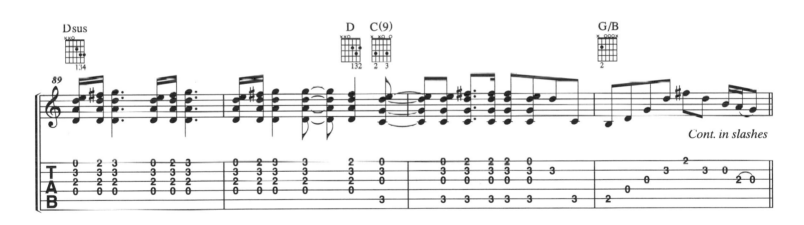

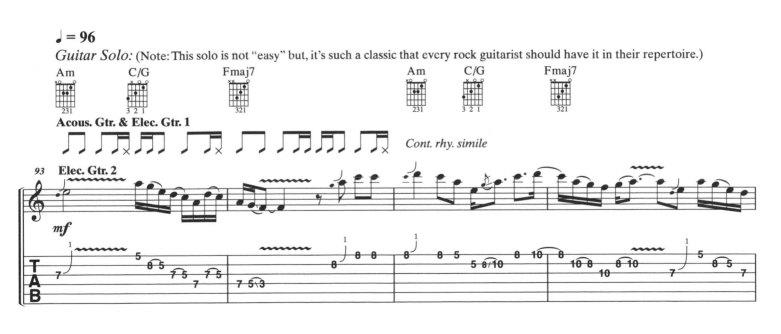

to be a rock___ and not to roll.___

And she's buy - ing a stair - way___ to heav - en.___

Soul Man

"Soul Man" was vocal duo Sam & Dave's biggest hit—a track that charged up to No. 2 on *Billboard*'s Hot 100 and topped the R&B Singles chart. Released on the Stax record label, the song was written by Stax's in-house songwriting team of Isaac Hayes and David Porter. "Soul Man" had a second wind when John Belushi and Dan Aykroyd included a version of the song in their 1980 cult movie, *The Blues Brothers*.

Take
Note

Guitarist Steve Cropper is known for his sliding 6th licks, and the opening of "Soul Man" is the definitive example. The sixteenth notes and triplet in the intro make this section look more complicated than it really is; Cropper is merely sliding a simple shape up and down the fretboard. In the following example, the stripped-down shapes are shown directly beneath each of the opening four measures. Notice how they're all fingered exactly the same way—with your middle finger on the 3rd string and your ring finger on the 1st string. Practice sliding the shapes on the second line until you're comfortable, then try it in rhythm, as shown on the top line.

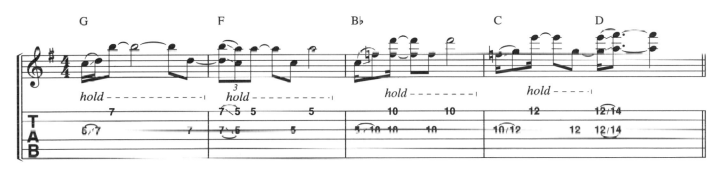

Once the song kicks into gear, Cropper plays a melodic line with chords by moving small shapes around on the top three strings. This happens pretty quickly, so you'll need to find an efficient way of fingering these chords. Instead of playing the full G barre chord shown in the chord frame, try barring your index finger across the top three strings at the 3rd fret, and add your middle and ring fingers to the 3rd and 4th strings, respectively, for a four-string G chord. With this formation, you can access the other three chord shapes by simply sliding the barre up and down while moving your middle finger around (or leaving it off for the barre at the 5th fret).

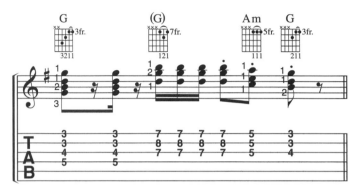

When the song changes keys in measure 31, Cropper moves his sliding 6th shape to follow the new chords. Use the same fingering here that you used in the opening section.

DEFINITION

The sliding 6ths in the intro of "Soul Man" are more generally known as **intervals**. An interval is the distance between two notes. To find an interval, move up a major or minor scale and count the notes. For instance, your starting note is "1," the next note is "2," and so on, so the distance between the first and second note is a 2nd. When you reach the sixth note, the interval between that note and the first note is a 6th. It's important to remember that *both* notes—the starting note *and* the ending note—are included in your count.

☆ **FUN FACT** ☆

The Stax Records house band played behind Sam & Dave on "Soul Man." Featuring Booker T. Jones on keyboards, Steve Cropper on guitar, Duck Dunn on bass, and Al Jackson, Jr. on drums, the group laid down the music behind a host of other hits on the Stax label, including tracks by Otis Redding, Wilson Pickett, Albert King, and others. Also known as Booker T & the MG's, they were a successful band in their own right, recording classic songs like "Green Onions."

Soul Man

Words and Music by
ISAAC HAYES and DAVID PORTER

Cont. in notation

Give you hope and be your on-ly boy - friend,_ yeah,_ yeah, yeah, yeah!

I'm talk-in' a-bout a

Elec. Gtr.

hold hold hold hold

Chorus:

soul man. I'm a soul man. Andyou, soul man.

Repeat ad lib. and fade

Soul man. Oh no,_ soul man._ I'm a soul man. Andyou a

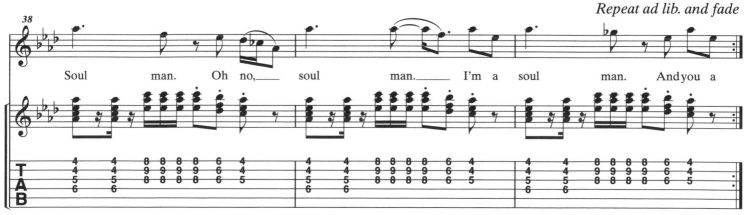

Verse 2:
Got what I got the hard way.
And I'll make it better each and every day.
So, honey, now, don't you fret, heh,
'Cause you ain't seen a-nothin' yet.
(To Chorus:)

Verse 3:
I was brought up on a side street.
Listen, now, I learned to love before I could eat.
I was educated at Woodstock.
When I start lovin', oh, I can't stop.
(To Chorus:)

Sunshine of Your Love

Key Thoughts

Cream is widely recognized as the first true rock supergroup—a band formed by musicians already recognized as superstars in their own right. The band had a knack for finding the perfect riff, and the riff to "Sunshine of Your Love" may be their most famous.

Take Note

"Sunshine of Your Love" begins with a stripped-down version of the riff. When you listen to the recording, you'll notice that the notes have a low, thick sound, even though they are in a relatively high range for a riff of this type. The fullness of the sound comes from playing these notes on low strings up around the 10th fret. If you were to play the same notes in first position, you'd get a much weaker, thinner tone. To really nail Clapton's sound, you also need to add a wide vibrato to the F note by rapidly bending the string towards the floor and returning. The opening two bars are shown below, with a wavy symbol over the F to indicate the vibrato.

After the initial single-line statement of the riff, Clapton fattens it up by playing the first four notes as power chords and the last three notes an octave higher. The riff has gone from a one-dimensional linear melody to suddenly having a low bottom end (from the power chords) and a striking high end (the high octave ending).

☆ FUN FACT ☆

After deciding "Sweet 'n' Sour Rock 'n' Roll" just wasn't quite the right name for them, the band went with "Cream" instead. It was a much more appropriate name for the trio, who were considered to be the "cream of the crop" amongst blues and jazz musicians in the British music scene.

Sunshine of Your Love

Words and Music by
JACK BRUCE, PETE BROWN
and ERIC CLAPTON

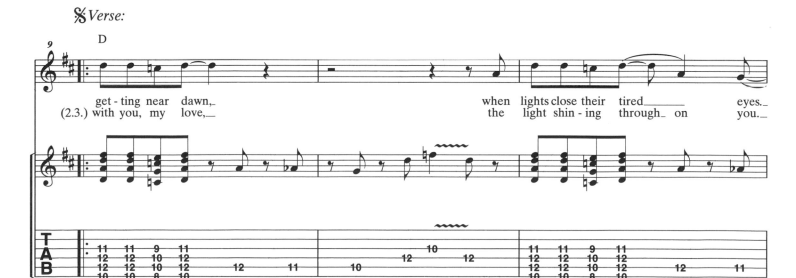

With Arms Wide Open

Key Thoughts

Creed followed up their multi-platinum debut record, *My Own Prison*, with another blockbuster—*Human Clay*. By this time, they had already had several hits, but "With Arms Wide Open" was the first to crack No. 1 on *Billboard*'s Hot 100. A rocking ballad, "With Arms Wide Open" helped ensure Creed was not a flash in the pan, holding *Human Clay* on *Billboard*'s Top 200 album chart for 101 weeks, and winning a Grammy for Best Rock Song.

Take Note

Make sure to tune your guitar down to Drop D tuning (D–A–D–G–B–E) for "With Arms Wide Open." The chord symbols in the opening measures make the beginning look more complicated than it is; if you look closely, though, you'll notice that these measures use mostly open strings, with fretted notes only on the 2nd and 5th strings throughout. Fret the bass walk-down from C to B with your ring and middle fingers, leading to the open A string. This leaves your index and pinky fingers available to fret the melodic embellishments on the 1st and 3rd frets of the B string. Fingerpick this part, assigning your thumb, index, middle, and ring fingers to the 5th, 4th, 3rd, and 2nd strings, respectively.

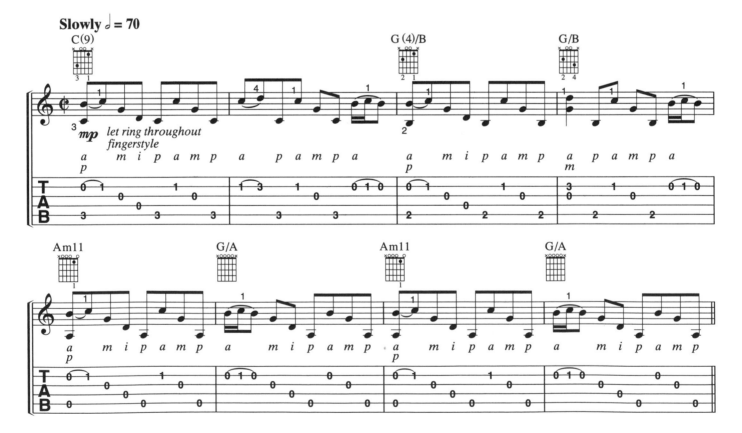

One advantage of playing in Drop D tuning is that it allows you to play one-fingered *power chords* by barring your index finger across the bottom three strings (below, left). Guitarist Mark Tremonti uses these shapes for the A5 and B♭5 chords behind the guitar solo and bridge. Adding your ring and pinky fingers to this shape creates a huge-sounding power chord (below, right). Tremonti employs this shape in the choruses for the E5 and F5 chords.

One-Finger Power Chord Shape

Extended Power Chord Shape

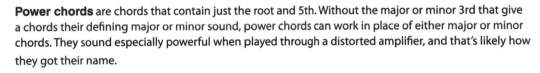

DEFINITION

Power chords are chords that contain just the root and 5th. Without the major or minor 3rd that give a chords their defining major or minor sound, power chords can work in place of either major or minor chords. They sound especially powerful when played through a distorted amplifier, and that's likely how they got their name.

In the seventh measure of the guitar solo, extra notes are used under the melody to thicken the lick. If you have trouble switching from single notes to chords, just drop the bottom two notes of each chord and play the melody on the 3rd string. It'll sound fine.

☆ **FUN FACT** ☆

Creed self-produced their debut record, *My Own Prison*, on a shoe-string budget. Reports claim they got it done for as little as $6,000—a startlingly low number, given that the record went platinum several times over and produced multiple hit songs.

With Arms Wide Open

Gtr. tuned in Drop D:
⑥ = D   ③ = G
⑤ = A   ② = B
④ = D   ① = E

Words and Music by
MARK TREMONTI and SCOTT STAPP

Slowly ♩ = 70

C(9)   G (4)/B   G/B

mp let ring throughout
fingerstyle

Am11   G/A   Am11   G/A

1. Well,

Verse:

C   G6/B

Play rhy. slashes on repeats

I   just   heard   the news   to-day.   It
I   don't   know   if I'm   read-y   To

Rhy. Fig. 1

1st time only

Whole Lotta Love

Key Thoughts

To create this unique and timeless rock classic, Jimmy Page and Robert Plant seamlessly fit the lyrics of Willie Dixon's song "You Need Love" to a relentless three-note guitar/bass riff and a powerful drum performance. "Whole Lotta Love" was the lead-off track to Led Zeppelin's second album and their only song to crack the top ten in the U.S.

Take Note

It is vital to play this riff with conviction and a bit of a swagger. The words "delicate" or "polite" do not belong in any conversation about "Whole Lotta Love." This song is all about attitude!

Remember to incorporate alternate picking (down- and up-strokes) when playing this riff. When counting sixteenth notes in $\frac{4}{4}$, we usually count "1–e–&–a, 2–e–&–a, 3–e–&–a, 4–e–&–a." Down-strokes would come on the downbeat and "&" of each beat, and up-strokes would come on the "e" and "a" in between.

The riff in "Whole Lotta Love" includes a *pickup*, which means the lick starts before the beginning of the first measure. The pickup is counted "&–a, 4–e–&," with the note on "4" tied to the previous note, and is picked "down–up–up–down."

There's a very cool little trick used in this pickup. Begin the riff by sliding your 3rd finger on the 6th string from the 5th fret to the 7th fret. Then, with your index finger, bend the 5th string up very slightly while you strike the open 4th string at the same time. The dissonance between the open D and the slightly out-of-tune bent D produces a fat, funky noise that makes a single D note sound wimpy and inadequate by comparison.

The riff is picked with straight down- and up-strokes until the 3rd beat, where there's a reiteration of the pickup from the very beginning. Notice that the downbeats do not have a *palm mute*, but the E notes on the open 6th string are dampened with the fleshy part of your picking hand.

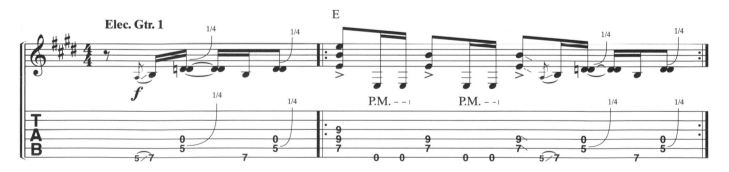

DEFINITION

The **palm mute** is a technique in which the fleshy part of your picking hand lightly touches the strings and dampens the sound to produce a percussive effect with a less-distinct pitch.

The guitar solo that starts in measure 21 is definitely not easy but is included as an option if you're up to the challenge. Otherwise, just play the rhythm guitar chords.

There is a minor variation of the riff in the outro. On alternate passes, the riff ends with a slide up to A on the 12th fret of the 5th string and resolves down to G♯ at the 11th fret on the following beat.

☆ **FUN FACT** ☆

This rather suggestive song was selected by British officials to represent the U.K. in the closing ceremony of the 2008 Olympics. It was performed by Jimmy Page atop a double-decker bus.

GUITAR GODS

A youthful **JIMMY PAGE** began his musical career as an in-demand session musician in London and played on many well-known records of the mid- to late-1960s. In 1966, he was recruited to replace the bassist in the Yardbirds and played alongside his friend Jeff Beck. As more members of the band left, Page moved back to guitar and filled the vacancies with John Paul Jones (bass), Robert Plant (vocals), and John Bonham (drums). The band originally called themselves the New Yardbirds, but changed their name to Led Zeppelin—based on an off-the-cuff remark by The Who's drummer, Keith Moon. Fluent in many styles of guitar from heavy blues-rock to acoustic folk, Jimmy Page assumed the producer's role and maintained creative control of Led Zeppelin for the duration of the band's lofty flight.

Whole Lotta Love

Words and Music by
JIMMY PAGE, ROBERT PLANT,
JOHN PAUL JONES, JOHN BONHAM
and WILLIE DIXON

Verse 2:
You've been learning, and, baby, I been learning.
All them good times, baby, baby, I've been yearning.
Way, way down inside, honey, you need.
I'm gonna give you my love.
I'm gonna give you my love.
(To Chorus:)

Verse 3:
You've been cooling, and, baby, I've been drooling.
All the good times, baby, I've been misusing.
Way, way down inside, I'm gonna give you my love.
I'm gonna give you every inch of my love.
I'm gonna give you my love.
(To Chorus:)

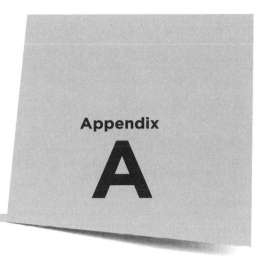

Chord Theory

You don't have to understand the music theory of chord construction to play the songs in this book. The notation, TAB, and chord diagrams tell you everything you need to know to play the music correctly. Someday, though, you're bound to find music that doesn't give you as much information as we have, and you'll need to know at least a little bit about chords to get it right. This section should help you out in those situations, and also add some basic chops to your knowledge of music.

Intervals

Play any note on the guitar, then play a note one fret above it. The distance between these two notes is a *half step*. Play another note followed by a note two frets above it. The distance between these notes is a *whole step* (two half steps). The distance between any two notes is referred to as an *interval*.

In the example of the C major scale on the following page, the letter names are shown above the notes, and the *scale degrees* (numbers) of the notes are written below. Notice that C is the first degree of the scale, D is the second, and so on.

The name of an interval is determined by counting the number of scale degrees from one note to the next. For example, an interval of a 3rd, starting on C, would be determined by counting up three scale degrees, or C–D–E (1–2–3). C to E is a 3rd. An interval of a 4th, starting on C, would be determined by counting up four scale degrees, or C–D–E–F (1–2–3–4). C to F is a 4th.

Intervals are not only labeled by the distance between scale degrees, but by the *quality* of the interval. An interval's quality is determined by counting the number of whole steps and half steps between the two notes of that interval. For example, C to E is a 3rd. C to E is also a *major* 3rd because there are 2 whole steps between C and E. Likewise, C to E♭ is a 3rd. C to E♭ is also a *minor* third because there are 1½ steps between C and E♭.

There are five qualities used to describe intervals: *major, minor, perfect, diminished,* and *augmented*.

Interval Qualities

Quality	Abbreviation
major	M
minor	m
perfect	P
diminished	dim or °
augmented	aug or +

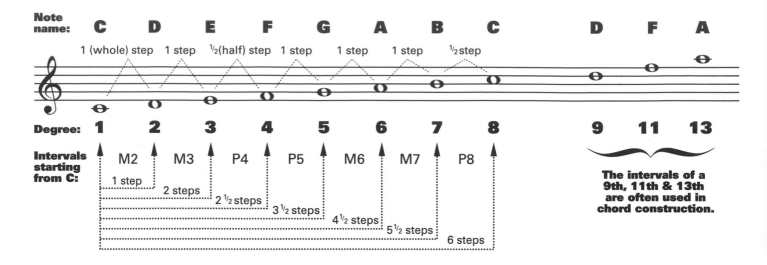

Particular intervals are associated with certain qualities. Not all qualities pertain to every type of interval, as seen in the following table.

Interval Type	Possible Qualities
2nd, 9th	major, minor, augmented
3rd, 6th, 13th	major, minor, diminished, augmented
4th, 5th, 11th	perfect, diminished, augmented
7th	major, minor, diminished

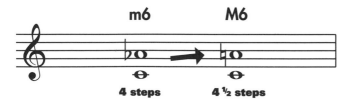

When a major interval is made smaller by a half step, it becomes a minor interval.

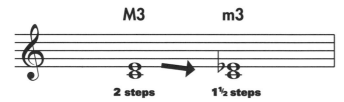

When a minor interval is made larger by a half step, it becomes a major interval.

When a perfect or minor interval is made smaller by a half step, it becomes a diminished interval.

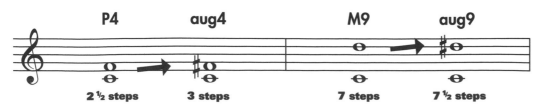

When a perfect or major interval is made larger by a half step, it becomes an augmented interval.

Following is a table of intervals starting on the note C. Notice that some intervals are labeled *enharmonic*, which means that they are written differently but sound the same (see aug2 and m3).

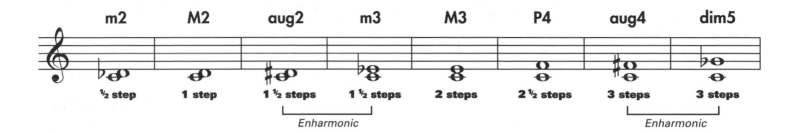

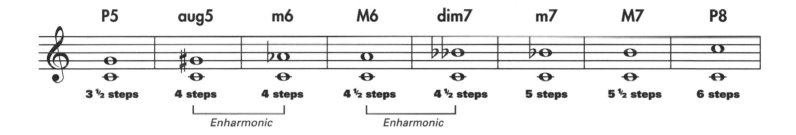

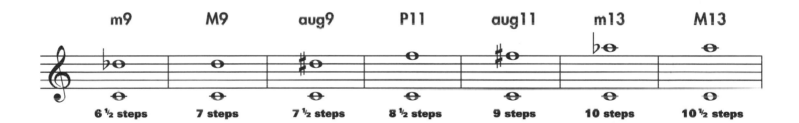

Basic Triads

Two or more notes played together are called a *chord*. Most commonly, a chord will consist of three or more notes. A three-note chord is called a *triad*. The *root* of a triad (or any other chord) is the note from which a chord is constructed. The relationship of the intervals from the root to the other notes of a chord determines the chord *type*. Triads are most frequently identified as one of four chord types: *major, minor, diminished,* and *augmented*.

Chord Types

All chord types can be identified by the intervals used to create the chord. For example, the C major triad is built beginning with C as the root, adding a major 3rd (E) and adding a perfect 5th (G). All major triads contain a root, M3, and P5.

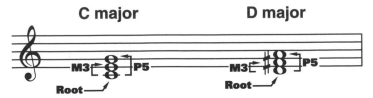

Minor triads contain a root, minor 3rd, and perfect 5th. (An easier way to build a minor triad is to simply lower the 3rd of a major triad.) All minor triads contain a root, m3, and P5.

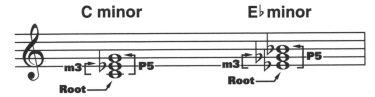

Diminished triads contain a root, minor 3rd, and diminished 5th. If the perfect 5th of a minor triad is made smaller by a half step (to become a diminished 5th), the result is a diminished triad. All diminished triads contain a root, m3, and dim5.

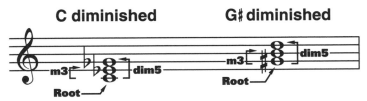

Augmented triads contain a root, major 3rd, and augmented 5th. If the perfect 5th of a major triad is made larger by a half step (to become an augmented 5th), the result is an augmented triad. All augmented triads contain a root, M3, and aug5.

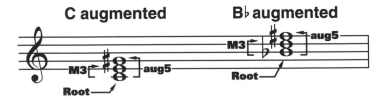

Chord Inversions

An important concept to remember about chords is that the bottom note of a chord will not always be the root. If the root of a triad, for instance, is moved above the 5th so that the 3rd is the bottom note of the chord, it is said to be in the *first inversion*. If the root and 3rd are moved above the 5th, the chord is in the *second inversion*. The number of inversions that a chord can have is related to the number of notes in the chord: a three-note chord can have two inversions, a four-note chord can have three inversions, etc.

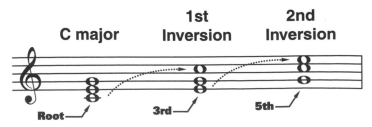

Building Chords

By using the four chord types as basic building blocks, it is possible to create a variety of chords by adding 6ths, 7ths, 9ths, 11ths, and so on. The following are examples of some of the many variations.

So far, the examples provided to illustrate intervals and chord construction have been based on C. Until you're familiar with chords, the C chord examples on the previous page can serve as a guide for building chords based on other notes. For example, to construct a G7(♭9) chord, you can first determine what intervals are contained in C7(♭9) and use the steps below to build the same chord starting on G.

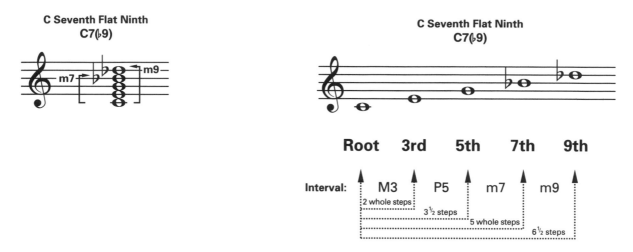

- First, determine the *root* of the chord. A chord is always named for its root, so G is the root of G7(♭9).

- Count *letter names* up from the *letter name of the root* (G) to determine the intervals of the chord. Counting three letter names up from G to B (G–A–B, 1–2–3) is a 3rd, G to D (G–A–B–C–D) is a 5th, G to F is a 7th, and G to A is a 9th.

- Determine the *quality* of the intervals by counting half steps and whole steps up from the root. G to B (2 whole steps) is a major 3rd, G to D (3½ steps) is a perfect 5th, G to F (5 whole steps) is a minor 7th, and G to A♭ (6½ steps) is a minor 9th.

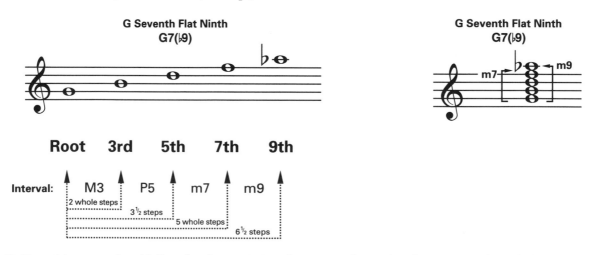

Follow this general guideline for determining the notes of any chord. As intervals and chord construction become more familiar to you, you'll be able to create original fingerings on the guitar. Don't be afraid to experiment!

The Circle of Fifths

The *circle of fifths* will help to clarify which chords are enharmonic equivalents (yes, chords can be written enharmonically as well as notes). The circle of fifths also serves as a quick reference guide to the relationship of the keys and how key signatures can be figured out in a logical manner. Moving clockwise (up a P5) provides all of the sharp keys by progressively adding one sharp to the key signature. Moving counter-clockwise (down a P5) provides the flat keys by progressively adding one flat to the key signature.

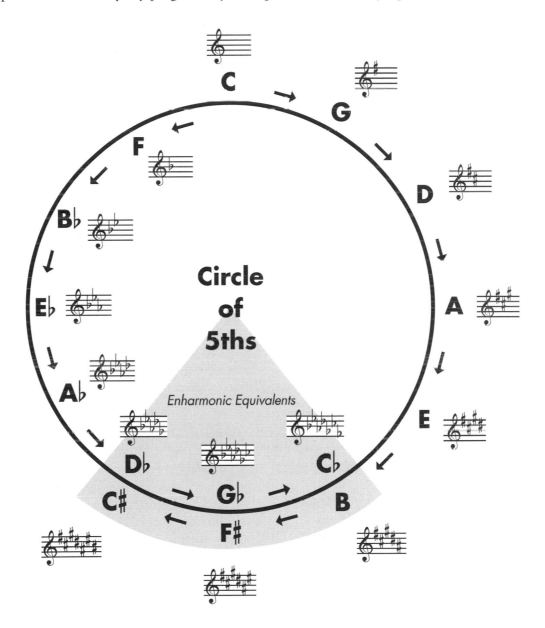

Chord Symbol Variations

Chord symbols are a form of musical shorthand that provide you with as much information about a chord as quickly as possible. The intent of using chord symbols is to convey enough information to recognize the chord, yet not so much as to confuse the meaning of the symbol. Chord symbols are not universally standardized and are written in many different ways—some are easy to understand, others are confusing. To illustrate this point, following is a list of some of the variations copyists, composers, and arrangers have created for the more common chord symbols.

C	**Csus**	**C(♭5)**	**C(add9)**	**C5**	**Cm**
C major	Csus4	C-5	C(9)	C(no3)	Cmin
Cmaj	C(addF)	C(5-)	C(add2)	C(omit3)	Cmi
CM	C4	C(♯4)	C(+9)		C-
			C(+D)		

C+	**C°**	**C6**	**C6/9**	**Cm6/9**	**Cm6**
C+5	Cdim	Cmaj6	C6(add9)	C-6/9	C-6
Caug	Cdim7	C(addA)	C6(addD)	Cm6(+9)	Cm(addA)
Caug5	C7dim	C(A)	C9(no7)	Cm6(add9)	Cm(+6)
C(♯5)			C9/6	Cm6(+D)	

C7	**C7sus**	**Cm7**	**Cm7(♭5)**	**C7+**	**C7(♭5)**
C(addB♭)	C7sus4	Cmi7	Cmi7-5	C7+5	C7-5
C7̶	Csus7	Cmin7	C-7(5-)	C7aug	C7(5-)
C(-7)	C7(+4)	C-7	C⌀	C7aug5	C7̶-5
C(+7)		C7mi	C ½dim	C7(♯5)	C7(♯4)

Cmaj7	**Cmaj7(♭5)**	**Cm(maj7)**	**C7(♭9)**	**C7(♯9)**	**C7+(♭9)**
Cma7	Cmaj7(-5)	C-maj7	C7(-9)	C7(+9)	Caug7-9
C7̶	C7̶(-5)	C-7̶	C9♭	C9♯	C+7(♭9)
C△	C△(♭5)	Cmi7̶	C9-	C9+	C+9♭
C△7					C7+(-9)

Cm9	**C9**	**C9+**	**C9(♭5)**	**Cmaj9**	**C9(♯11)**
Cm7(9)	C$^9_7$	C9(+5)	C9(-5)	C7̶(9)	C9(+11)
Cm7(+9)	C7add9	Caug9	C7$^9_{-5}$	C7̶(+9)	C(♯11)
C-9	C7(addD)	C(♯9♯5)	C9(5♭)	C9(maj7)	C11+
Cmi7(9+)	C7(+9)	C+9		C9̶	C11♯

Cm9(maj7)	**C11**	**Cm11**	**C13**	**C13(♭9)**	**C13($^{♭9}_{♭5}$)**
C-9(♯7)	C9(11)	C-11	C9addA	C13(-9)	C13(-9-5)
C(-9)7̶	C9addF	Cm(♭11)	C9(6)	C$^{13}_{♭9}$	C(♭9♭5)addA
Cmi9(♯7)	C9+11	Cmi7$^{11}_9$	C7addA	C(♭9)addA	
	C7$^9_{11}$	C-7($^9_{11}$)	C7+A		

Reading Chord Frames

Guitar chord frames are diagrams that show the fingering and position of a particular chord on the neck of the guitar. Vertical lines represent the strings, and horizontal lines represent the frets. Dots on the diagram show exactly where to place the fingers, and corresponding numbers at the bottom of the frame tell which fingers to use.

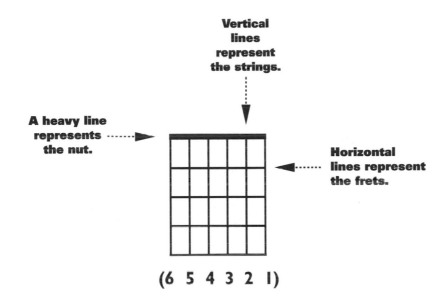

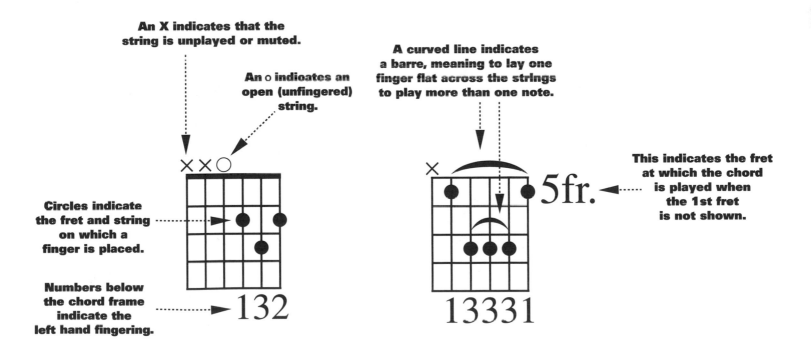

Guitar Fingerboard Chart

Frets 1–12

STRINGS

6th 5th 4th 3rd 2nd 1st
E A D G B E

FRETS		STRINGS					
		6th	5th	4th	3rd	2nd	1st
← Open →		E	A	D	G	B	E
← 1st Fret →		F	A#/Bb	D#/Eb	G#/Ab	C	F
← 2nd Fret →		F#/Gb	B	E	A	C#/Db	F#/Gb
← 3rd Fret →		G	C	F	A#/Bb	D	G
← 4th Fret →		G#/Ab	C#/Db	F#/Gb	B	D#/Eb	G#/Ab
← 5th Fret →		A	D	G	C	E	A
← 6th Fret →		A#/Bb	D#/Eb	G#/Ab	C#/Db	F	A#/Bb
← 7th Fret →		B	E	A	D	F#/Gb	B
← 8th Fret →		C	F	A#/Bb	D#/Eb	G	C
← 9th Fret →		C#/Db	F#/Gb	B	E	G#/Ab	C#/Db
← 10th Fret →		D	G	C	F	A	D
← 11th Fret →		D#/Eb	G#/Ab	C#/Db	F#/Gb	A#/Bb	D#/Eb
← 12th Fret →		E	A	D	G	B	E

Fretboard note names:

1st Fret: F B♭ E♭ A♭ C F / A# D# G#
2nd Fret: F#/G♭ B E A D♭/G♭ / C# F#
3rd Fret: G C F B♭ D G / A#
4th Fret: G#/A♭ C#/D♭ F#/G♭ B E♭/A♭ / D#/G#
5th Fret: A D G C E A / G#
6th Fret: A#/B♭ D#/E♭ G#/A♭ C#/D♭ F B♭ / A#
7th Fret: B E A D G♭/B / F#
8th Fret: C F B♭ E♭ G C / A# D#
9th Fret: C#/D♭ F#/G♭ B E A♭/D♭ / G# C#
10th Fret: D G C F A D
11th Fret: D#/E♭ G#/A♭ C#/D♭ F#/G♭ A#/B♭ D#/E♭
12th Fret: E A D G B E

Glossary

accent   Emphasis on a beat, note, or chord.

accidental   A sharp, flat, or natural sign that occurs in a measure.

altered tuning   Any tuning other than standard tuning on the guitar.

arpeggio   The notes of a chord played one after another instead of simultaneously.

backbeats   In $\frac{4}{4}$ time, beats 2 and 4 in a measure. In most types of rock and pop music, the drummer usually accents the backbeats by hitting the snare, giving the music a strong feeling of forward momentum.

bar   See *measure (or bar)*.

bar line   A vertical line that indicates where one measure ends and another begins.

barre   To fret multiple strings with one finger.

barre chord   A chord played by fretting several strings with one finger.

bend   A technique of pushing a guitar string up or down with the fretting finger to change the pitch.

bridge   The part of the guitar that anchors the strings to the body.

brush stroke   To lightly strum the guitar strings with the index finger of the right hand.

capo   A device placed around the neck of the guitar to raise the pitch of the strings.

chord   A group of three or more notes played simultaneously.

chord progression   A sequence of chords played in succession.

common time   The most common time signature found in music; there are four beats to every measure and the quarter note gets one beat. Same as $\frac{4}{4}$.

countermelody   A melody played at the same time as the main melody.

cut time   A time signature that usually indicates a faster tempo where there are two beats to every measure and the half note gets one beat. Same as $\frac{2}{2}$.

distortion   An electronic effect that alters the sound of an amplified instrument by distorting the signal. Compared to overdrive, distortion produces a higher level of signal alteration or "fuzz."

dotted note   A note followed by a dot, indicating that the length of the note is longer by one half of the note's original length.

double bar line   A sign made of one thin line and one thick line, indicating the end of a piece of music.

double stop   A group of two notes played simultaneously.

downbeat   The first beat of a measure.

down-pick   To pick the string downward, toward the floor.

down-stroke   To strike the strings downward, toward the floor.

down-strum   To strum the strings downward, toward the floor.

drop D tuning   An altered tuning in which the 6th string of the guitar is lowered from E to D.

economy of motion   A concept for efficient playing that involves moving as few fingers as little as possible when changing chords.

eighth note   A note equal to half a quarter note, or one half beat in $\frac{4}{4}$ time.

eighth rest   A rest equal to the duration of an eighth note.

enharmonic   Two notes of the same pitch, but with different names. For example, B♭ and A♯ are enharmonic notes.

fermata   A symbol that indicates to hold a note for about twice as long as usual.

fifth   The 5th note of a scale above the root note, the distance of seven half steps.

fingerboard   See *fretboard*.

fingerpicking   A style of playing that uses the right hand fingers to pluck the guitar strings rather than using a pick.

fingerstyle   To play the strings with the fingers rather than with a pick.

flat   A symbol that indicates to lower a note one half step.

fret   The metal strips across the fretboard of a guitar.

fretboard   The part of the guitar neck where the frets lay.

fuzz   An electronic effect that is one of the first guitar effects ever produced. The sound produced is an extremely high level of distortion.

G clef   See *treble clef.*

grace note   A small note played quickly either just before a beat or right on the beat.

groove   The sense of rhythm in a piece of music.

half note   A note equal to two quarter notes, or two beats in $\frac{4}{4}$ time.

half rest   A rest equal to the duration of a half note.

half step   The distance of one fret on the guitar.

hammer-on   A technique by which a note is made to sound after playing the string with the right hand by tapping down on the string with another finger of the fretting hand.

harmonics   The notes of the harmonic series that sound clear and bell-like when played, produced by lightly touching a string at various points on the fretboard and indicated in notation with diamond-shaped symbols.

harmony   The result of two or more tones played simultaneously.

Hertz (Hz)   The unit of measurement for the frequency of vibration.

interval   The distance in pitch between notes.

key   The tonal center of a piece of music.

key signature   The group of sharps or flats that appears at the beginning of a piece of music to indicate what key the music is in.

ledger lines   Short horizontal lines used to extend a staff either higher or lower.

major chord   A chord consisting of a root, a major 3rd, and a perfect 5th.

major scale   The most common scale in music, consisting of a specific order of whole and half steps: W–W–H–W–W–W–H.

major third   A note that is four half steps up from the root.

measure (or bar)   Divisions of the staff that are separated by bar lines and contain equal numbers of beats.

minor chord   A chord consisting of a root, a minor 3rd, and a perfect 5th.

minor third   A note that is three half steps up from the root.

mode   A set of notes arranged into a specific scale.

mute   To stop a note from ringing on the guitar by placing either the right or left hand over the strings.

natural   A symbol that indicates a note is not sharp or flat.

note   A symbol used to represent a musical tone.

nut   The part of the guitar at the top of the neck that aligns the strings over the fretboard.

octave   The interval between two immediate notes of the same name, equivalent to 12 frets on the guitar, or eight scale steps.

open E tuning   An altered tuning for the guitar in which the strings are tuned from low to high E–B–E–G♯–B–E.

open G tuning   An altered tuning for the guitar in which the strings are tuned from low to high D–G–D–G–B–D.

open position   Fingering for chords that incorporates open strings and no barre.

overdrive   An electronic effect that alters the sound of an amplified instrument by slightly distorting the signal. Overdrive produces less signal alteration than distortion.

palm mute   A technique of muffling the guitar strings with the right hand palm at the bridge of the guitar.

palming the pick   A technique of holding the pick in the palm of the hand with the ring finger, while keeping the index and middle fingers free.

pendulum strumming   A technique in which you keep your arm moving up and down even if a strum is not indicated. The idea is keep a strong groove by not breaking strumming momentum.

pentatonic scale   A five-note scale.

pick   A device used to pluck or strum the strings of a guitar.

pickup   A device on the body of an electric guitar that converts the vibrations of the strings into electronic signals, enabling them to be amplified.

pima   Abbreviations for the right hand fingers in fingerpicking notation, in which p = thumb, i = index finger, m = middle finger, and a = ring finger.

pinch technique   A fingerpicking technique in which the right hand plucks two strings at once between the thumb and another finger.

pitch   The location of a note related to its lowness or highness.

position   The location of the hand on the fretboard at a particular fret.

power chord (or "5" chord)   A chord consisting of only the root and 5th, without a 3rd or other additional notes.

pull-off   A left hand technique in which two notes are fingered on the same string, and the lower note is then made to sound by pulling the fretting finger off the higher note.

quarter note   A note equal to one beat in $\frac{4}{4}$ time and the basic unit of musical time.

quarter rest   A rest equal to the duration of a quarter note.

repeat signs   A group of various symbols indicating sections of music to be played over again.

rest   A symbol representing measured silence in music.

rhythm   The musical organization of beats.

riff   A short, repeated melodic pattern.

root note   The fundamental note of a chord, and also the note that gives the chord its letter name. The root is the first note of the corresponding major scale.

scale   A set of notes arranged in a specific order of whole steps and half steps. The most common scale is the major scale.

sharp   A symbol that indicates to raise a note one half step.

shuffle rhythm   A rhythm in which eighth notes are played in an uneven, long-short manner.

sixteenth note   A note equal to half an eighth note, or one quarter beat in $\frac{4}{4}$ time.

sixteenth rest   A rest equal to the duration of a sixteenth note.

slash chord   A chord with a note other than the root in the bass. These are labeled with the chord name on the left, followed by a slash with the bass note listed to the right.

slide   1: A technique of moving smoothly from one note to another. A note is fingered by the left hand and played by the right hand, then the left hand finger maintains pressure while sliding quickly on the string to the next note without interrupting the sound or picking the note again. Indicated in notation with a diagonal line between notes. 2: A metal or glass tubing that fits over a left hand finger, used to fret the strings and produce slide notes.

staccato   To play notes in a short, distinct manner. Indicated in notation by a dot directly over or under the note or chord.

staff   The horizontal lines and spaces upon which music notes are placed to designate their pitch.

standard tuning   The normal tuning for the guitar in which the strings are tuned from low to high E–A–D–G–B–E.

strum   To play several strings by brushing quickly across them with a pick or the fingers.

swing   To play eighth notes in an uneven, long-short rhythm.

syncopation   A shift of rhythmic emphasis to the weak beat, or to a weak part of a beat.

TAB   Abbreviation for *tablature.*

tablature   A system of guitar notation that uses a graphic representation of the six strings of the guitar with numbers indicating which fret to play.

tempo   The speed at which music is played.

tie   A curved line that joins two or more notes of the same pitch, indicating to play them as one continuous note.

time signature   A sign resembling a fraction that appears at the beginning of a piece of music. The top number indicates how many beats are in each measure and the bottom number indicates what kind of note gets one beat.

tone control   An adjustable knob on the body of an electric guitar that controls the amount of treble, or high-frequency output.

treble clef   A symbol at the beginning of the staff that designates the second line as the note G. Also called the *G clef.*

tremolo bar   See *whammy bar.*

triplet   A group of three notes played in the time of two.

unison   The same pitch played at the same time on different strings of the guitar.

up-pick   To pick the string upward, toward the ceiling.

up-stroke   To strike the strings upward, toward the ceiling.

up-strum   To strum the strings upward, toward the ceiling.

vibrato   A rapid alteration of pitch slightly higher or lower than the main pitch, usually achieved by rapidly bending the string.

volume control   An adjustable knob on the body of an electric guitar that controls the overall output of the instrument.

whammy bar   A handle attached to the body of an electric guitar below the strings, used to alter the pitch of the strings by moving the bridge.

whole note   A note equal to four quarter notes, or four beats in $\frac{4}{4}$ time.

whole rest   A rest equal to the duration of a whole note, or the duration of any full measure.

whole step   The distance of two frets on the guitar.

The following blank chord frames may be used to keep track of new chords. Write them here as you learn so you won't forget them.

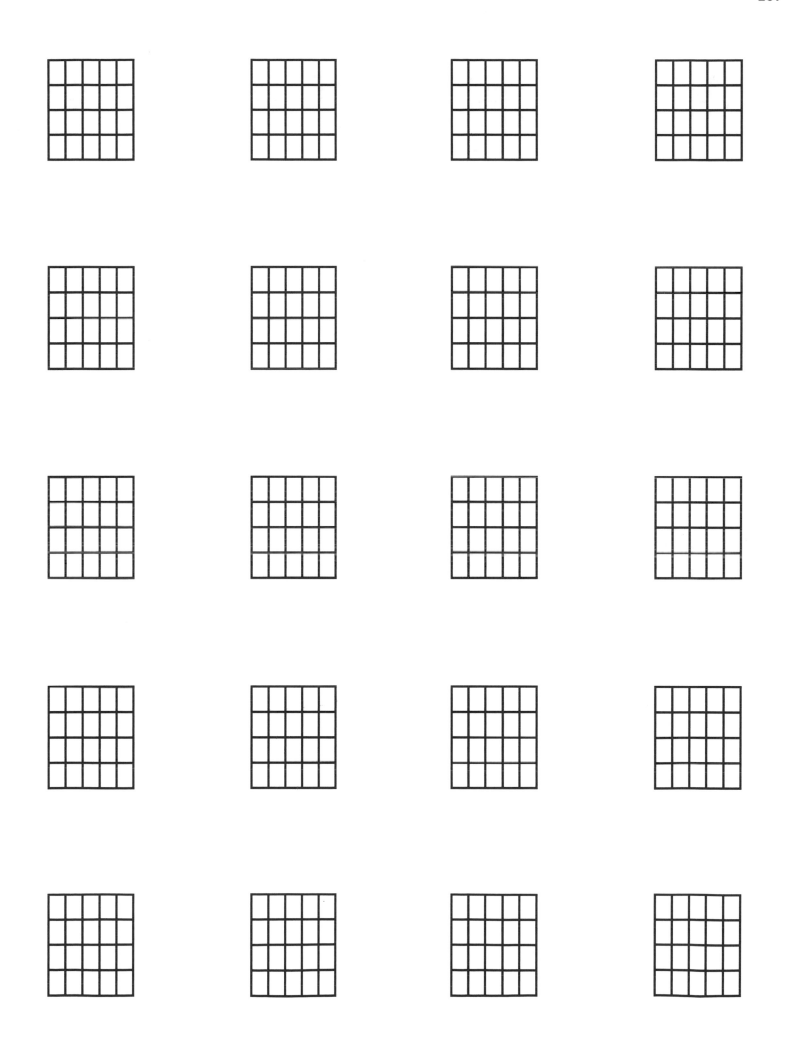